Of Course, You can Speak in Tongues!

Of Course, You can Speak in Tongues!

(PRACTICAL STEPS
TO FOLLOW)

Dr. John Seo

Copyright © 2016 Dr. John Seo

ISBN:13:9780692631188
ISBN:10:0692631186

Printed in the United States of America
2016 by CreateSpace

All rights reserved. No portion of this book may be used without permission of the publisher, with the exception of brief excerpts in magazine articles, reviews, books, etc.
Unless otherwise indicated, all Scriptures are taken from the New International Version of the Bible.

Preface

§

THE CURRENT MOVEMENT OF HOLY Spirit started in the early part of 20th century has spread fast unto four corners of the world as a wild fire and working wondrously through almost all Christian denominations in the world today.

At the beginning, the movement started in a mountain, in small churches, and in small meetings especially among low educated people, just as started in the Jerusalem church which was made of uneducated Galilean fishermen, almost 2000 years ago.

Today, all the people in the different classes of the society have experienced of the Baptism of the Holy Spirit and of the gift of speaking tongues.

They are the presidents of universities, deans of colleges, nuclear engineers, doctors of computer science, professors of physic and chemistry, psychologists, mathematicians, linguistic experts, oncology doctors, philosophers, historians, pilots, astronomers, biologists including plain citizens just like us.

Now many saints in the world have experienced the fullness of the Holy Spirit and the gift of speaking tongues and live wonderful lives in the Lord. Many of them work effectively as spiritual warriors for the kingdom of God using their spiritual gifts.

They are like Cornelius and his friends who were in the high class of the time (see Acts 10), received the fullness of the Holy Spirit and the gift of speaking in tongues through Peter.

Sudden experiences of the Holy Spirit, and sudden changes of the people's lives and attitudes have caused all kinds of noises and problems in the churches and among denominations.

In the worst case, some Christians think wrongly that speaking in tongues is given by Satan, even though the Bible never mentioned that case.

I like to give you an illustration in order to explain the problem more clearly. Let's look at the issue of gun control.

Today, in America we have social problems, and one of them is gun abuse. It is very shameful to search the bodies of students at high schools.

Small boys in middle school killed their teachers and class mates. The story became serious issues among the leaders of this country.

In the oriental countries, the laws do not allow regular citizens have guns. So they do not have gun accidents at all. But robbers have smuggled guns and threat innocent citizens and some times kill them.

Regular citizens can not protect themselves, and must depend on the police.

I am personally favor of eliminating guns in the society, but against total elimination of the weapons.

Think of soldiers who do not carry weapons and guns.

How American soldiers won the fight against Iraq?

Because of better weapons.

If American soldiers had fought without weapons against Iraqi soldiers in the middle East, they would have been beaten by enemies.

When soldiers use the weapons wisely and properly, the weapons are very good and useful.

Recently the weapons are used by stupid youngsters for the purpose of revenge and boosting their prides, and the weapons can cause all kinds of problems.

The Holy Spirit gave the gift of speaking tongues to Christian soldiers, but some of them do not read

"How to use" manual in 1 Cor. 14, and used the gift improperly, and became arrogant.

This kind attitude and wrong doing have troubled many Christians who did not have same experience and gifts.

Also, same blame goes to the people who were not baptized by the Holy Spirit.

John the Baptist said in the Gospel of John that God, the Father foretold him about Jesus.

John 1:33, I would not have known him, except that the one who sent me to baptize with water told me, 'The man on whom you see the Spirit come down and remain is he who will baptize with the Holy Spirit.' -NIV-

Acts 1:8, "But you will receive power when the Holy Spirit comes on you; and you will be my witnesses in Jerusalem, and in all Judea and Samaria, and to the ends of the earth."

God gave the gifts of the Holy Spirit to the Christian soldiers so that they can fight well against Satan and his angels.

A sad story is that Christian soldiers are fighting one another.

They are so foolish and blind that they do not know they are irritated by Satanic power.

God gave the gifts to protect and support the body of Jesus Christ, the church, but parts of the body fight hard trying to destroy the body and hurting one another.

God is very sad.

They are arguing, fighting, and saying unprofitable words.

Matt 12:36-37, "But I tell you that men will have to give account on the day of judgment for every careless word they have spoken. For by your words you will be acquitted, and by your words you will be condemned."

1 Peter 4:5, But they will have to give account to him who is ready to judge the living and the dead.

Not many Christians know what is the worst sin in the world.

The worst sin in this world is to be against the body of Jesus, the church.

Some Christians treat other Christians as children of Satan.

It is very serious sin. Christians who already received the gifts of the Holy Spirit should be humble, nice, and use the gifts properly so that the church may be benefited.

Christians who do not receive the gifts of the Holy Spirit also should be humble, not jealous, and try to solve the problem that block the flow of the spiritual gifts.

Regardless the gifts, we are Christians, brothers and sister, and the children of God, through Jesus Christ, the only Redeemer who gives His life for us.

Someday we will go to Father's house and we will stand before the Almighty God. Then we do not need any gift.

> **1 Cor 13:8-13, But where there are prophecies, they will cease; where there are tongues, they will be stilled; where there is knowledge, it will pass away. For we know in part and we prophesy in part, but when perfection comes, the imperfect disappears... Now I know in part; then I shall know fully, even as I am fully known. And now these three remain: faith, hope and love. But the greatest of these is love.**

So, do not fight one another. One has one gift and another has another gift.

God loves us all when we are humble and work hard as the members of the one body, only for the Glory of God.

I am writing this book for the purpose of encouraging and advising the usage of the gifts of the Holy Spirit in the fight against Satan and his kingdom.

I pray that all Christian soldiers in the world live very victorious lives in the guidance of the Holy Spirit.

This book is based upon mostly experiences and true testimonies for laymen instead of doctrinal discussion or apologetic debate on certain Scriptures.

First, I thank God who has been with me, protected, and blessed me always even though I did not quite notice His providence.

Without his guidance, it is impossible for me to write this book. I praise His name.

Secondly, I thank my better half who is a Christian SEAL, and spiritual Green Beret, who walks with me always. She is a wonderful helper in the Lord.

Thirdly, I like to thank Christian brothers and sisters who have encouraged our Spanish mission works with financial helps and prayers during our 6-year Latin America mission works.

I like to give special thank to Mrs. Maureen Green who edited and proofread the manuscripts with the Love of God and with the passion for the Glory of His Kingdom.

In the Peace and Grace of the Lord, John Seo

Contents

Preface v

Chapter 1 Introduction of Speaking in tongues ... 1
Chapter 2 Beginning of language 7
Chapter 3 Meaning of Speaking in tongues 15
Chapter 4 Gift of Speaking in tongues 20
Chapter 5 Kinds of tongues 27
Chapter 6 How could they Speak in tongues in
           the early churches? 34
Chapter 7 What are the benefits of Speaking in
           tongues? 48
Chapter 8 Reasons why people can not speak in
           tongues. 70

Chapter 9	Preparations for Speaking in tongues. · 77
Chapter 10	Deeper truths · 86

About the Author · · · · · · · · · · · · · · · · · 125
Reference Books · · · · · · · · · · · · · · · · · 127

CHAPTER 1

Introduction of Speaking in tongues

I think every Christian can speak in tongues. It is not just my word. I got this conviction after 40 years of study. The eternal Word of God had told us a wonderful promise.

1 Cor 14:5, "I would like every one of you to speak in tongues,"

God encourages us to speak in tongues, because He is ready to give to all of us.

However, some Christians raise questions, quoting,

1 Cor 12:30, "Do all have gifts of healing? Do all speak in tongues?"

Today, many Christians think that the gift of speaking in tongues is given only to certain people.

They simply do not understand God's true intention.

The two scriptures above seemed contradict each other. But there is no contradiction if you read the contents very carefully.

Let me give you give an illustration so that you can easily understand.

When God created human beings, He made man with the ability to swim. Surely, He wants all men to be able to swim, as most of the animals do, from ant, to the elephant. That was God's intention.

Do all men swim today? No! Some people do not like to swim, because they are afraid of deep water.

Some Africans who live a primitive life in plains of deep land do not have river nor lake, cannot swim.

Some family members who even own their own swimming pool, but do not like to swim.

Two or three years old babies normally cannot swim.

Likewise, all Christians can speak in tongues, but some of them refuse to do so, or do not know how to receive the gift of speaking tongues.

Mark 16:17-18, and these signs will accompany those who believe: In my name they will drive out demons; they will speak in new tongues;

Speaking in tongues was one of signs given to the believers.

Alas, there are many benefits you can get when you speak in tongues.

I am going to introduce one of them here.

A Prayer for unknown future!

There is a story I heard long time ago from Dr. Paul Cho who was the senior pastor of the largest church in the world, during his revival meeting in a Korean church in San Francisco.

This was when Dr. Cho was teaching at Full Gospel Bible College in Seoul, Korea.

One day he was heading toward a class room to teach a morning class to the students.

Suddenly he felt his heart compelled by the Holy Spirit to pray immediately. He hesitated a little bit, but he obeyed and returned to his office, and prayed aloud by speaking in tongue.

After he got a peace in his heart, he returned to his class. Of course, he was late at his class teaching.

Dr. Cho had a brother who lived in a rural area.

His brother, Mr. Cho planned to come to Seoul that day.

It was long time ago, and at that time the country was poor and there were only few buses per day that went between the rural area and Seoul.

Mr. Cho had waited for quite a while for the bus bound for Seoul, and finally the bus came, but it was over crowded with not a single seat available.

He tried hard to push himself inside the bus and he had almost succeeded.

Suddenly someone pulled him down. Mr. Cho was very angry and looked back trying to find out who pulled him down. He saw an old man with white hairs.

Ignoring this old man, Mr. Cho tried hard to get inside the bus, but again he was pulled down by the same man.

When he got down on the ground, the bus left. Mr. Cho was very upset. He would have to wait a few hours for the next bus.

He tried to shout to this old man, but when he looked back, to his surprise, he couldn't see anybody.

After few hours of angry emotion, and many disturbing questions about this old man, the next bus came, and he got on the bus.

On his way to Seoul, his bus stopped at the highest point of the hill, and he saw through the bus windows, that there were many police cars and ambulances.

He asked the spectators on the road what happened and found out that the bus he had tried so hard to get on, had gone over the side and rolled many times into the valley and crushed, and all passengers were killed.

When he came to see Dr. Cho in Seoul, Mr. Cho told the story and talked about the mystery old man.

Dr. Cho asked his brother immediately.

"Brother!, What time was it when you tried to take the first bus?"

"It was about 10 o'clock."

"That is it! My God! This morning at 10 o'clock I prayed in tongues."

Because of the prayer Dr. Cho made, God sent an angel and saved the life of Mr. Cho.

We do not know what will happen even in a minute. But the Holy Spirit who knows the future, asks our spirits to pray for the events which will occur and God will protect us by answering our prayers.

Tongue speaking prayer can save us from future accidents and tragedies!

When you have read this book, I hope you will speak in tongues, the gift of the Holy Spirit.

Furthermore, with your abundant life led by the Holy Spirit, you will accomplish the will of God in this world, as it was done before in Heaven.

1 Cor 2:10, but God has revealed it to us by his Spirit. The Spirit searches all things, even the deep things of God.

With all the saints whom we have helped in speak in tongues, my wife and I like to give big hands of thanksgiving and praise, to the Holy Spirit.

The Holy Spirit is wonderful God, and He always keep the promises made by Jesus, God, the Son and the God, Father.

Eternal glory to our God!

CHAPTER 2

Beginning of language

A BABY LEARNS HOW TO speak from his parents. We know a true story:

A boy taken away and raised by a wolf, later cried out just like a wolf.

The children born in the United States of America speak in English. But some of them speak only Chinese or a different tongue because their parents taught only their mother tongue.

In Gen. 2:7, the Bible tells us how God created the first man, Adam. God formed man of the dust of the ground, and breathed into his nostrils the breath of life; and man became a living soul.

The word *soul* in Hebrew is nephesh, meaning "an animated, *breathing*, conscious, and *living* being."

Man did not become a *living* soul until *God* breathed life ...

Do you think God created Adam as a baby?

I don't think so. Possibly God created the first Adam about Thirty-three years old--a man, as Jesus Christ our Lord who lived until thirty-three years old. About that age, a man can grow up to perfect physical condition during his life.

There are many testimonies of spiritual Christians who had been in heaven, share with us the story that they had seen all believers who had previously died looked like young people in their 30s or younger.

In heaven, Enoch who was taken by God at the age of 365 does not look a lot younger than his son, Methuselah who died at the age of 969 years.

When God breathed into his nostrils the breath of life, Adam received the inner image of God, including conversational language.

John 20:22, ...and with that he breathed on them and said, "Receive the Holy Spirit."

God was going to the same thing to the disciples of Jesus as He did to Adam. In a word, when they received the Holy Spirit, they also received conversational languages, also called "TONGUES."

God commanded Adam not to eat the fruit of the knowledge of good and evil. God commanded this because Adam could understand what God said.

When Adam saw Eve for the first time, Adam said;

Gen 2:23, The man said, "This is now bone of my bones and flesh of my flesh;"

Because of the fall of man, Adam and Eve were cast out of the Garden of Eden.

Their first son, Cain slew his brother Abel, and answered back to the question of God.

Gen 4:9, Then the Lord said to Cain, "Where is your brother Abel?"

"I don't know," he replied. "Am I my brother's keeper?"

Certainly they could communicate with God.

After Noah's flood, people of the world were multiplied by the three sons of Noah.

Gen 11:1, Now the whole world had one language and a common speech.

In the land of Shinar, people were building a city and tower in order to reach up to heaven; and to make them a name, and lest they be scattered abroad upon the face of the whole earth.

They did not want any interference by God, such as the flood of Noah.

They wanted to be liberated and tried to exclude God from their lives.

When they reached to the acme of humanism, God confounded their language and scattered people.

Gen 11:8-9, So the Lord scattered them from there over all the earth, and they stopped building the city. That is why it was called Babel, because there the Lord confused the language of the whole world. From there

the Lord scattered them over the face of the whole earth.

Since that time, there have been many nations and tribes in this world. Today there are about 6,000-7,000 languages being used.

They all have their own languages.

After the destruction of Tower of Babel, could any tribe use the same language used between God and Adam? Was it Hebrew? I don't know.

In order to help further understandings of tongues, let's look at the three different activities of the Trinity throughout the human history.

In the Old Testament time, God, the Father was understood as God who mainly controlled the world, and He did from the heaven above.

In the New Testament time, Jesus, God the Son mainly worked in this world. He was among us as His name meant "IMMANUEL."

Fifty days after the resurrection of Jesus Christ, our Lord, God, the Holy Spirit came upon the disciples of Jesus, as Jesus promised.

The Holy Spirit came and dwelled inside of the bodies of the disciples and Christians.

Now "the humanism" at the tower of Babel had finished and started "the individual theocracy."

1 Cor 3:16, "Don't you know that you yourselves are God's temple and that God's Spirit lives in you?"

The Holy Spirit is the Lord of our body, and He likes to use His language. That's why He gives us the gift of speaking in tongues. It is a new language we do not understand.

Acts 2:4, All of them were filled with the Holy Spirit and began to speak in other tongues as the Spirit enabled them.

The language used between men and God was lost because of the sin at The Tower of Babel.

New languages (or unknown languages) could be used through the grace of the second Adam, Jesus, when the Holy Spirit came to the disciples as Jesus promised.

It was a historic moment when the curtain for a new era of salvation and new communication was opened for all Christians by pouring out the spiritual gifts.

Among the nine spiritual gifts in 1 Cor. 12, all gifts except speaking in tongues and tongue interpretation can be found in the Old Testament, through

Moses, Joshua, Samuel, David, Solomon. Elijah, Elisha and other prophets God had used many gifts.

In the Old Testament, God gave us a prophecy in **Isa 28:11, "Very well then, with foreign lips and strange tongues God will speak to this people …"**

Only speaking in tongues and tongue interpretation were given to the believers since the Pentecost. They are very special, but today ignored among Christians.

Praise the Lord, if you speak in tongues!

Christians who do not speak in tongues will praise God because they will speak in tongues before they finish or after reading this book.

Especially when they follow the instruction mentioned in this book.

Praise the Lord!

In Acts 2:16-21, Peter said, "No, this is what was spoken by the prophet Joel:

'In the last days, God says, I will pour out my Spirit on all people.

Your sons and daughters will prophesy, your young men will see visions, your old men will dream dreams.

Even on my servants, both men and women, I will pour out my Spirit in those days, and they will prophesy.

I will show wonders in the heaven above and signs on the earth below, blood and fire and billows of smoke.

The sun will be turned to darkness and the moon to blood before the coming of the great and glorious day of the Lord.

And everyone who calls on the name of the Lord will be saved.'"

CHAPTER 3

Meaning of Speaking in tongues

For anyone who speaks in a tongue does not speak to men but to God. Indeed, no one understands him; he utters mysteries with his spirit. -1 Cor 14:2-

TONGUE IS DEFINED AS A part of body in the mouth and also as language. Webster's Third New International Dictionary defines that tongue is;

A. a spoken language, a speech used by a particular people or class or in a particular region.
B. a language other than one's own: a foreign or strange language.

It's Greek counterpart is "Glossia" that means "language."

In I Cor 14:2, For anyone who speaks in a tongue does not speak to **men** but to **God.** Indeed, **no one** understands him; he utters mysteries **with his spirit.**

The language which can be used to tell his secrets to God can not be understood by himself nor by bystanders, including angels and evil spirits.

Only his spirit and God know the contents of speaking in tongues.

Some one can raise a question such as:

"Why do we need such language, if we pray silently?"

When we commit sins in mind and thoughts, we can repent without saying any audible voice.

But, when we commit sins by saying audible words, we'd better to confess with audible words.

Words, especially spoken words are very powerful and effective.

When Jesus died on the cross, he was very tired and exhausted. Still he said last seven words aloud enough that his followers could hear.

In the 4th chapter of book of Matthew, we see the story of temptation of Jesus in the wilderness. When he was tempted, Jesus answered back.

Matt 4:4, Jesus answered, "It is written: 'Man does not live on bread alone, but on every word that comes from the mouth of God.'"

All the words of God in the Bible are truth. But by the helps of the Holy Spirit, they become living words proceeding out of the mouth of God now.

Then they perform miracles, and they are good for our spiritual life, as bread is to our physical body.

Whether it is God's or man's, spoken words are very powerful. As an example we see;

Rom 10:9-10, "That if you confess with your mouth, Jesus is Lord, and believe in your heart that God raised him from the dead, you will be saved. For it is with your heart that you believe and are justified, and it is with your mouth that you confess and are saved."

Without confession (with audible voice), it is impossible to get salvation. Spoken words are very important in Christian, and spiritual life.

Most of Korean Christians pray together with loud voices during day break prayer meetings (every day) and over night prayer meetings at Friday nights.

Some times they pray aloud during Sunday morning services.

Today many Christians in America pray silently and pray very short prayers. There is no way they can grow spiritually well.

Spoken prayers and confessions are very important in the spiritual world.

James 5:16, "Therefore confess your sins to each other and pray for each other so that you may be healed. The prayer of a righteous man is powerful and effective."

Jer 33:3, "Let your cry come to me, and I will give you an answer, and let you see great things and secret things of which you had no knowledge."
-BBE-

It is impossible to call unto God silently!

When God created the world, he used his powerful words. We also use words, and words perform many things.

Today all the activities in the world are being done by words of men.

Tongues are languages. Some times they were written as *unknown* tongues in the Bible.

Because the speaker of the tongues are not supposed to understand. The speaker and persons around him can not understand! God wants that way.

In the old Greek text, there is no word "*Unknown*" before the words, "tongues."

Tongues in the Bible are not the sound of water, wind, thunder, shower, water fall, ocean wave, birds nor animals. Tongues are languages only his spirit and God understand. It is a very personal and secret conversation between them.

CHAPTER 4

Gift of Speaking in tongues

SPEAKING IN TONGUES IS ONE of nine spiritual gifts the Holy Spirit gave to the church of Corinth.

These spiritual gifts are general ones given to every body. A very common gift among Christians.

As our God is almighty, His gifts are countless.

James 1:16-17, "Don't be deceived, my dear brothers. Every good and perfect gift is from above, coming down from the Father of the heavenly lights . . ."

All the church members can have at least one gift, and one of them is speaking in tongues.

Through words, energy is transferred, works are done, and miracles are happened.

The gift, speaking in tongues is like a pipe through which other gifts from the heaven can flow into us.

We have the gift of language first, so we may request God for other gifts.

Speaking in tongue is a communication gift.

In 1 Cor. 12, the Bible says that the Lord Jesus gives differences of administrations, and God, the Father gives diversities of operations.

Then, the Holy Spirit gives nine spiritual gifts to the members of the church.

Jesus as the Son of God is in charge of administrations of the church such as bishop, pastor, elder, deacon, teacher, missionary, etc., and the Father is in charge of operations, such as natural phenomenon, wonders, signs, human history, etc.

Here, we see the trinity of God.

The nine spiritual gifts of the Holy Spirit can be divided into 3 groups. These gifts can be same kinds of talents a Christian has from his birth. But the gifts and talents can be compared to jewels vs stones.

a. Gifts of thoughts---word of wisdom, word of knowledge, discerning of spirit
b. Gifts of will----------faith, healing, miracles

c. Gifts of language---prophecy, speaking in tongues, interpretation of tongues

Gifts are like tools. God gives for us to use to edify the body of Jesus, the church. But the gift, speaking in tongues is given to edify individual person.

Whether he commits bad sins or not, God does not take away the gift of speaking in tongues once God gave it to him.

As long as he believe in Jesus as his Lord and Savor, he can use the gift until he die.

But other spiritual gifts can be taken back by God, when people use them for wrong purposes or misuse them.

There was a famous preacher in Korea. God gave him the healing gift to help sick refuges during Korean War. At that time the disease of tuberculosis was epidemic. People could not get proper medication, and many died.

The news of his healing miracles were spread rapidly by words of mouth, and hundreds sick people came in the house of the preacher. They stayed in every room including the bathroom, and they did not leave until cured completely.

During the war, food was scarce, but there was no family life or privacy for the preacher. He worked day and night healing the patients without enough food or sleep.

When he prayed in the Spirit, and put his right hand over the clothes, the patient was cured completely. His hand left burned mark on the body, like mark branded on the animals. Cured people left his house, and more sick people came.

One day he prayed God to take away the gift of healing from him, and God answered and took away the gift, and he no longer had the gift of healing.

Quite a few women who had received the gift of prophecy, used their spiritual gifts for making money as fortune tellers. God gave the gift to edify the local churches, but because of the way the gift was being used, God took away their gifts of prophecy.

1 Cor 14:4-5, He who speaks in a tongue edifies himself, but he who prophesies edifies the church.

In Acts we can find practices of Spiritual gifts.

Ananias talked with God in vision. Saul (Paul) saw in a vision a man, named Ananias coming in and putting his hands upon him.

Peter also had also a vision.

He became hungry and wanted something to eat, and while the meal was being prepared, he fell into a trance. He saw heaven opened and something like a large sheet being let down to earth by its four corners. It contained all kinds of four-footed animals, as well as reptiles of the earth and birds of the air. -Acts 10:10,11-

They had the gift of vision. Peter knew that Ananias and Sapphira told a lie. He has the gift of revelation.

Peter and John raised the lame. That was the result of practicing the gifts of healing and of faith.

In Acts 9:40, Peter made the dead body of Tabitha alive. I think Peter used the gifts of miracles and of faith together.

When Stephen preached the words of God, they were cut to the heart. Stephen had the gift of word of knowledge.

There are quite a few of example about prophecy in Acts.

Acts 21:9, He had four unmarried daughters who prophesied.

Acts 13:9-12, Then Saul, who was also called Paul, filled with the Holy Spirit, looked straight Elymas and said,

"You are a child of the devil and an enemy of everything that is right! You are full of all kinds of deceit and trickery. Will you never stop perverting the right ways of the Lord? Now the hand of the Lord is against you. You are going to be blind, and for a time you will be unable to see the light of the sun."

Immediately mist and darkness came over him, and he groped about, seeking someone to lead him by the hand. When the proconsul saw what had happened, he believed, for he was amazed at the teaching about the Lord.

Paul used the gifts of faith and miracles, and prophecy.

"God did extraordinary miracles through Paul, so that even handkerchiefs and aprons that had touched him were taken to the sick."
-Acts 19:11,12-

There were no special power in the handkerchiefs nor aprons. God commanded angels to heal them.

In the beginning of the scripture, it clearly says,

"God did extraordinary miracles."

Paul didn't do anything, but God.

God likes to give spiritual gifts to all the Christians who like to work for the Lord.

Also, there was Paul's sweat in the handkerchiefs and aprons that were in contact with Paul's body.

Acts 5:15-16: As a result, people brought the sick into the streets and laid them on beds and mats so that at least Peter's shadow might fall on some of them as he passed by. Crowds also gathered from the towns around Jerusalem, bringing their sick and those tormented by evil spirits, and **all of them were healed.**

Even Peter's shadow was a part of Peter and the healing was powerful.

Every good and perfect gift is from above, coming down from the Father of the heavenly lights, who does not change like shifting shadows.

-James 1:17,18-

When we work intentionally with the gifts of the Holy Spirit for the body of Jesus, we will bear the fruit of the Spirit as long as we are part of the body of Jesus.

Like branches to the tree vine, Are you ready to work for the Lord?

Then you can ask God for the gifts!

CHAPTER 5

Kinds of tongues

ACCORDING TO THE UNITED BIBLE Society, there are about 6000 to 7,000 languages in the world, and other noises such as whispering, various sounds are used to communicate thoughts, ideas or significance between more than two parities.

> **There are, it may be, so many kinds of voices in the world, and none of them is without signification. -2 Cor 12:4, KJV-**

In Acts 2, one hundred twenty followers of Jesus spoke in tongues. Sixteen different tongues were recognized by the Jews, who happened to be there from 16 different countries.

Then, how about the rest, 104 tongues? Nobody understood these utterances. The tongue speakers including stand-by couldn't understand at all.

They all spoke languages that were used other place outside Palestine area, on earth and in the heavens.

God doesn't want to expose the contents of secrete which speaker's spirit is saying to God.

So, the speaker himself and persons around him can not understand when the speaker speaks in tongues.

Tongues can be divided into two groups,

a. tongues in this world
b. tongues in spiritual world, and in heaven

In the first case, we see 7,000 tongues in this world.

Secondly we can see the tongues (languages) used between God and God's angels, and Satan and evil spirits.

> **But even the archangel Michael, when he was disputing with the devil about the body of Moses, did not dare to bring a slanderous accusation against him, but said, "The Lord rebuke you!**
> **-Jude 1:9, NIV-**

We do not know what language the Michael used, whether Hebrew or Aramaic.

Certainly the Michael used a language that Satan understood.

Also, there are languages used in heaven.

Paul mentioned in 1 Cor. 13:1,

"If I speak in the tongues of men and of angels,"

All tongues, known or unknown, in this world can be interpreted by the person who has the gift of tongue interpretation if God allows.

Therefore, the gift of tongue interpretation is given to a few Christians.

This is a true story I read from a book which testifies many miracles occurring during a man's mission trip to Russia.

With difficulty the permission for a crusade was allowed miraculously in one rural place in Russia, and the American preacher stood on the platform to preach. A Russian interpreter supposed to translate for him. The preacher did not know what the government officer would not allow the interpreter while he preached. The local government intentionally tried to prevent him from preaching the Gospel. The minister who did not know any Russian was very perplexed. For suddenly he preached the sermon in Russian! The Holy Spirit let him use Russian language!

When this author was ministering in San Diego, I met a young man, Mr. Han who came from one of richest family in the Choong Chung province in Korea.

During the conversation with me, he confessed the unusual mystery he could not understand for a long time. His family was very rich, so he could study in China, Japan, and came to the USA for further study.

In the summertime, the weather was hot even during night time. In the country there were no air-conditioning units, so they set a mosquito net on open wooden floor in the middle of the house.

This kind house has an entrance gate and open front yard. Winds can circulate through the house and make it cool.

One hot summer night, he was sleeping in the mosquito net on the wooden floor. It was very early in the morning 3 or 4 o'clock. When he was waken by some noise.

He saw an old servant sneak out of her room and quietly remove house gate lock and went out of the house.

With a great curiosity, he followed her very carefully. Then he saw her entering into one of the barns, he continued to follow her.

The old lady was praying on her knees.

When Mr. Han has heard the prayer, he was scarred to death. She was praying in Chinese, and in Japanese.

He ran away from the spot and did not talk to anyone about this mystery. How does this old lady speak in two foreign languages fluently?

Mr. Han knew her from his early childhood, and she did not have any formal education at all.

He asked me how it could be possible.

I explained that every thing is possible for God, and by the gifts of speaking in tongues.

I quoted Scriptures from the Bible. We prayed together, and at that time he received the Holy Spirit and he began to speak in tongues he never heard and understood. Hallelujah!

But God allows seldom the interpretations of tongues of <u>spiritual world</u> or <u>in heaven.</u>

Paul mentioned about these:

How he was taken up into Paradise, and words came to his ears which may not be said, and which man is not able to say. -2 Cor 12:4-

There are many languages (tongues) in this world, and God surely understand all languages when people use them for prayers.

The Holy Spirit gives the tongue-interpretation gift to a interpreter so that he can interpret the contents of the tongues. That way the person who spoke in tongue understands the mystery of the contents of the tongue and can be edified. Most of new tongue speakers have doubt with regard to the real necessity of speaking tongues because they do not know the contents of what they speak.

God gives the gift of tongue interpretation only to the person who is very prudent, and can keep the secret of people who speak secret things to God, Father.

Not only that the tongue interpreter can not remember for very long, the contents of what he interpreted. It is God's will to keep the contents of the prayer by tongue speaker, secret as much as possible.

My wife had received, the gifts of speaking tongue, of tongue interpretation, of prophecy, and of healing at a revival meeting led by one of the most spiritually powerful ministers in Korea.

She has interpreted the contents of tongue speaking for 40 years.

Through many experiences, we see that Holy Spirit generally allow the tongue interpreter to interpret the contents of the person's spiritual prayer including one's dedication for His Kingdom and Glory.

CHAPTER 6

How could they Speak in tongues in the early churches?

IN THE BOOK OF ACTS, we see three ways how they could receive the gift of tongues.

a. When they prayed

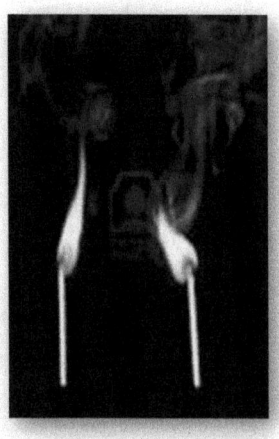

There were at least 500 followers of Jesus according to 1 Cor. 15:6, after the resurrection of Jesus. Probably they were on the mount of Olive when Jesus ascended into heaven leaving a wonderful promise with them.

On one occasion, while he was eating with them, he gave them this command:

"Do not leave Jerusalem, but wait for the gift my Father promised, which you have heard me speak about. For John baptized with water, but in a few days you will be baptized with the Holy Spirit." -Acts 1:4,5-

Only out of 120 people, 24% out of 500 truly believed and obeyed what Jesus said, and assembled.

They were all in one accord in one place.

They waited for the promise Jesus made.

They, including 12 disciples of Jesus already had believed in Jesus including Mary, the mother of Jesus, and his brothers.

Therefore I tell you that no one who is speaking by the Spirit of God says, "Jesus be cursed," and no one can say, "Jesus is Lord," except by the Holy Spirit. -1 Cor. 12:3-

> **Simon Peter answered, "You are the Christ, the Son of the living God." -Matt. 16:16-**
>
> **Jesus replied, "Blessed are you, Simon son of Jonah, for this was not revealed to you by man, but by my Father in heaven. -Matt. 16:17-**

Simon Peter believed in Jesus by the help of the Holy Spirit. But he was **not baptized** yet by Holy Spirit until Pentecost.

All believers were not baptized by the Holy Spirit when they first believed in Jesus.

> **When they arrived, they prayed for them that they might receive the Holy Spirit, because the Holy Spirit had not yet come upon any of them; they had simply been baptized into the name of the Lord Jesus. -Acts 8:15-17-**

The Christians in Samaria believed in Jesus with the help of the Holy Spirit and after then they were baptized in the water in the name of Jesus, Lord, but they were not baptized by the Holy Spirit (full of the Holy Spirit).

Because of their own personal experiences, they thought that the Holy Spirit came down from heaven.

All believers have the Holy Spirit inside them, but, when the moment they invite the Holy Spirit to the throne of their heart fully by denying his own will and humble themselves before the feet of Jesus Christ, the Holy Spirit begins to control whole body and they experience the baptism of the Holy Spirit.

In other words, when they give up their dominion over themselves and give up the throne in their minds, Holy Spirit can control 100% of his soul, and the moment it is called "the baptism of Holy Spirit."

Dying to our flesh we will be resurrected with Jesus Christ (Holy Spirit), we can live an abundant life.

John 10:10, I am come that they might have life, and that they might have it more abundantly.

-KJV-

The lives of Christians with full of Holy Spirit are different from the lives of regular Christians who have only eternal life.

In Act 2, when they prayed together fervently expecting the gift of Holy Spirit, they received the Holy Spirit and the gift of speaking tongues.

120 tiny small fires can cause a big fire.

About 35 years ago, one of Korean pastors in San Francisco Bay area, named Rev. Yoon wanted to receive the gift of speaking tongue. At that time, most of them had the gift of speaking tongues through very strong Holy Spirit movement led by many spiritual pillars in Korea.

Rev. Yoon was 2-3 years older than the rest of them, and hesitated to ask them putting their hands on him and pray for the gift.

So, either before or after Sunday, he placed his van in the quiet places, and had prayed aloud for a long time (over night), and finally one day he experienced the fullness of the Holy Spirit, and got the gift of speaking tongues.

He had a personal Pentecost event. But when believers **pray** together for the receiving of the Holy Spirit and gift of tongue speaking, they can receive more easily than only one Christian on his own.

b. When Peter preached

Acts 10:1-8, At Caesarea there was a man named Cornelius, a centurion in what was known as the Italian Regiment. He and all his family were devout and God-fearing; he

> gave generously to those in need and prayed to God regularly.
>
> One day at about three in the afternoon he had a vision. He distinctly saw an angel of God, who came to him and said, "Cornelius!"
>
> Cornelius stared at him in fear. "What is it, Lord?" he asked.
>
> The angel answered, "Your prayers and gifts to the poor have come up as a memorial offering before God. Now send men to Joppa to bring back a man named Simon who is called Peter.
>
> He is staying with Simon the tanner, whose house is by the sea."
>
> When the angel who spoke to him had gone, Cornelius called two of his servants and a devout soldier who was one of his attendants. He told them everything that had happened and sent them to Joppa.

One day an angel appeared when Cornelius was praying, and told him to invite Peter, to hear what he would say.

They would have conversed **in Greek, Latin** or **Hebrew** in his vision.

So the centurion, Cornelius sent his servants and a soldier to Peter who was in Joppa.

God knew where Peter stayed and gave the exact information as to how to find him.   Without a GPS gadget God knows where you are right now, and where you will be tomorrow.

His full name was Simon Peter

He was in Joppa, a seaport.

He was a guest in the home of a leather tanner, named Simon who lived by the sea.

No way they could miss the house!

God did not use Google maps!

Cornelius called his family members and close friends together and waited for the arrival of Peter.

When he greeted Peter, he fell down at his feet, and worshipped him.

At that time, Cornelius was a centurion of the so-called, "Italian Regiment", elite soldiers at that time of Roman Empire. They enforced and were the law in Palestine at that time. They could even get away with do bad, and wicked things if they wanted to.

They could be very arrogant, since they were special agents in the occupied territory under the control of Roman empire.

But Cornelius was different. He was a very humble man. That's why God gave him a chance to be baptized in the Holy Spirit, and to speak in tongues for the first time among Gentiles.

God likes to give His grace to the persons who are humble and honor Him. He invited his relatives and close friends.

When Peter preached the Gospel of Jesus Christ, all were baptized by the Holy Spirit and they all spoke in tongues.

The circumcised believers who had come with Peter were astonished that the gift of the Holy Spirit had been poured out even on the Gentiles. For they heard them speaking in tongues and praising God. -Acts 10:45, 46-

As soon as these gentiles believe in Jesus Christ, they received the gift of the Holy Spirit even without water baptism.

Please pay your special attention to this scripture,

" For they heard them speaking in tongues and praising God"

Peter and some of the believers from Joppa knew that all the gentiles in the place received the Holy Spirit, because they heard them speak with tongue;

Therefore speaking tongue is a clear evidence of receiving of the Holy Spirit. (Baptism of the Holy Spirit)

In Acts 3:4, "**All**" of them were filled with the Holy Spirit and began to speak in other tongues as the Spirit enabled them. We see the word "**All**."

Also we see the word "**All**" in "While Peter was still speaking these words, the Holy Spirit came on **all** who heard the message."

God of Grace likes to give His gifts to every Christian, specially the communication tool, the gift of speaking in tongues.

When Peter, the apostle with mighty power of the Holy Spirit preached the word of God, they all received the gift of the Holy Spirit.

Very strong fire at one house, can easily spread to other houses.

When Peter, a spiritually powerful disciple, **preached** the Gospel to the gentiles they received the Holy Spirit and the gift of speaking tongues.

c. When Paul laid on hands

On hearing this, they were baptized into the name of the Lord Jesus. When Paul placed his hands on them, the Holy Spirit came on them, and they spoke in tongues and prophesied. There were about twelve men in all.
-Acts 19:5-7-

In Ephesus, Paul found some disciples, and asked a question,

"Did you receive the Holy Spirit when you believed?"

The Bible says that they were believers. But they answered,

"No, we have not even heard that there is a Holy Spirit."

Here we see again, when Paul put his hand upon them and prayed, then **all** received the gift of the Holy Spirit.

As soon as they believe in Jesus Christ correctly, and when Paul laid his hands, they began to speak in tongues.

Verse. 7 says, "There were about twelve men in **all**."

This method, "putting hands on the head" is used very commonly today at the churches or at the revival meetings.

Can any minister lay on hands, pray, and make people speak in tongues?

I don't think so. Not all names of the disciples were mentioned in Acts except, Peter, John and Paul.

Only the ministers who can impart the spiritual gift have the duty and privilege of laying hands for the spiritual gifts.

Paul had that kind of special gift of Holy Spirit.

Rom 1:11, "I long to see you so that I may impart to you some spiritual gift to make you strong…"

Through our experiences, all the people whose head I had laid hands on, spoke tongues, when they wanted the gift sincerely, humbly and specially they obeyed to the spiritual authority.

I think, the ministers who lay on hands, and Christians help other people by holding hands, should be full of the Holy Spirit.

I can compare laying on hands to the electrical wire or cable. If the wire is as pure as gold, silver, copper, electricity flows fast in that order.

If the wire is big, the power would flow more. If the wire between the God and a believer is pure, big, and flexible (humble), full power is flowing down fast.

So, if the minister were pure, broad minded, and humble, the power of the Holy Spirit would be mighty and powerful.

All ministers who have the gift of speaking in tongues should make themselves ready and should try laying on hands.

They will find out the results soon.

Without trying and testing, no body knows he has a special gift from the Holy Spirit!

It is a good time to check one's talent, ability and condition.

For this reason I remind you to fan into flame the gift of God, which is in you through the laying on of my hands. -2 Tim 1:16-

Can the person who has the gift of tongue interpretation, interpret always?

He can interpret only what the Holy Spirit reveals.

The secretes of Christians are involved, so God allows only a few people interpret tongues.

God allows interpretation mainly of the contents of adoration, praising, and self-dedication parts.

Few people hear in their language when people speak in tongues. This case is very exceptional.

In most cases, the interpreters understand in their heart when people speak in tongues.

So, remember that tongue interpretation is not translation of spoken words (tongues).

They understand the spiritual meanings of the contents of tongues, and clearness of the interpretations are depend on the education, the capability of linguistic expression, and the faith of the interpreter.

The contents of tongues are at a very high level of expression that even the speaker is very illiterate.

When kindergartners or elementary school kids speak in tongues, their interpreted prayers are much better, beautiful, and artistic than prayers made by Ph.Ds. It is amazing.

For this reason anyone who speaks in a tongue should pray that he may interpret what he says.
-1 Cor. 14:13-

If you speak in tongues for decades, you understand generally what your spirit prays.

That way you may start to interpret.

CHAPTER 7

What are the benefits of Speaking in tongues?

◊

OUR MIND IS COMPOSED OF conscious and sub-conscious parts.

Various kinds of thoughts including sins, guilt, sorrow, worries, hatred, jealousy, complains, grudge, impure thinking, wicked imaginations, and other vices have been dumped into the mind.

Some of them we are able to remember (5-10%), and the most of them (90-95%) have sunken down to the sub-conscience level and piled up there for ages.

When we confess with our mouth, we confess to God only 5-10 % of our sins. From 90 to 95% of the sins stay intact in the sub-conscious. All the sins we committed without realizing it go to the sub-conscious.

a. First, persons who can speak in tongues have the privilege to confess 100% of his sins in conscious and sub-conscious.

That is the reason why the Holy Spirit gives us the gift of speaking in tongues in order to confess all our sins and be forgiven.

Therefore, persons who received the gifts of speaking in tongues, and of vision at the same time, could see a screen on which God could show the scenes of past committed sins from their early ages to present time. So, they repented over days and nights continually.

After repenting in tongues, every one feels that they can fly in the air, because all sins are forgiven and all burdens are lifted.

The world of conscious and sub-conscious can be compared with an iceberg.

God likes to keep the secrets, but some time reveals in order to eliminate sins and problems of the church.

This a true story I heard from Rev. Chun Suk Lee who is with the Lord now.

He was one of Korea's mighty spiritual leaders who had been full of the Holy Spirit, and had many spiritual gifts including tongues-interpretation.

A church in a Southern Korean village invited him for a revival meeting. So, from Seoul, he went down to the rural area by a train.

He was greeted by the pastor of that church, and they went to the church by way of country bus which took a long time. On their way, the pastor told Rev. Lee the reason why he was invited. Main reason was not for the revival of the church., there was another reason.

The church had two deacons who had been raised together in the village. They were very close friends and lived like brothers. As they had served the church faithfully and they both became deacons.

They were pillars for that church.

One day, when they were alone at home, one asked the other to loan a $5,000 and he would repay until certain date. He was desperate for the funds for his business. The other deacon prepared $5,000 bank loan by putting a lien on his house, and gave it to his friend.

The borrower asked, "Brother, do you want me write a promise note with my signature?"

The other deacon answered back, said, "NO! It is between you and me. I do not need any paper."

Time had gone by. But there was not any word from his friend about the loan.

Finally the other deacon asked his friend to pay back the loan, but the deacon said,

"what loan are you talking about?"

The deacon denied that he had received the money, and asked him to show the promise note as proof.

They became enemies. Also, the church members were divided into two groups who believed in one deacon and who believe in the other deacon.

The situation was really bad, and the pastor couldn't solve the problem at all. So, with prayers and meditations, he invited Rev. Chun Suk Lee to help resolve the problem. Even Solomon's wisdom seemed unable to solve the problem.

On the first day of the revival meeting, Rev. Lee asked two deacons to be seated in the two chairs on the pulpit.

During the revival meeting all in the audience felt the presence of the Holy Spirit and they began to speak in tongues including two deacons on the pulpit.

Rev. Lee who could interpret tongues heard one deacon on the pulpit started speaking in tongues.

The deacon cried aloud,

"I am thief! I am thief! I stole $5,000 from my best friend deacon."

So, Rev. Lee hit him on his head with his Bible,

"You are liar, and thief!" and demanded him to confess before the congregation, and he did with tears.

He promised to pay back the money, and confessed his sin before the congregation. The revival meeting was very successful by the help of the Holy Spirit.

b. When you speak in tongues, you can pray a long time.

Do we often quit speaking in tongues, because we do not understand what we pray? Yes, many Christians do.

Paul gave us an answer to this question about 2000 years ago.

So what shall I do? I will pray with my spirit, but I will also pray with my mind; I will sing with my spirit, but I will also sing with my mind.

-1 Cor 14:15-16-

Paul suggested us to pray in tongues and in our own language. A few spiritual Christians who have been praying in tongues for many years, generally know the contents of prayers by his spirit, therefore they pray in tongues instead of praying with their mind.

Prayer is a communication between God and us, and can be illustrated as follows.

The author was a ROTC Signal Corps officer in Korea and stationed in front of the DMZ.

There were two basic communication methods between the front line and the division headquarter.

One was telephone and the other was wireless radio.

Consider the method of telephone as prayer with a known language, and wireless radio is prayer in tongues.

Wired Telephone

<u>Advantage</u>

1. Sound is very clear, easily understood

<u>Disadvantages</u>

1. Very difficult to install (mountain, river, mine field, snow, flood, obstacles)
2. Once line is broken, very difficult to repair
3. Easily wiretapped by an enemy

Wireless Radio

Advantages

1. Very easy to install
2. You can communicate at any time without disturbance or wire-tapping by an enemy

Disadvantages

1. Cannot understand the contents without secret codes

It is very difficult to install telephone wires in the battle field, over mountains, under rivers, and especially in a mine field.

Once the line is installed, both parties can communicate easily.

The advantage of telephone is the clarity of the sound. Also both parties clearly understand what they say and hear.

But during mortar explosions and heavy snow, or flooding, the line can be easily broken, and it is very hard to find the broken place and repair it.

This is one of disadvantages of telephone. Furthermore, the line can be wiretapped easily by the enemy. Strategic plans discussed on the phone can be used by the enemy, and bring devastate results to our side.

That is why in Armed forces use wireless radio.

It is very easy to install whenever they want. They use secret codes so enemy cannot understand.

With your own language you can pray at certain places and certain times. The environment must be ready for your prayer. Once the prayer is stopped, it is not easy to resume.

In the stadium with the shouts of 40,000 people, it is almost impossible to pray in your language, but possible to pray in tongues. You can speak in tongues anywhere, whenever you want to pray, while dishwashing, driving car, even studying.

Rev. Choi, the mother of Dr. Paul Cho once was seen praying in tongues while she was sleeping.

There are many spiritual giants who spend a lot of time in praying in tongues, some for as long as 10-20 hours.

Oral Robert, Kenneth E. Hagin, and many spirit filled preachers are famous in their practice of speaking in tongues.

The commandment in the Bible, "pray without ceasing" is possible only if you pray in tongues.

1 Thess 5:17, **Pray without ceasing.** -KJV-

You can pray as long as you want, 2 hours, 10 hours, or whole day.

c. We pray in tongues according to the will of God.

When we pray in our languages, some times our prayers are not what they should be.

When you ask, you do not receive, because you ask with wrong motives, that you may

spend what you get on your pleasures. -James 4:3-

But when we speak in tongues, we pray according to the will of the Holy Spirit and pray very high dimensional ones.

And he who searches our hearts knows the mind of the Spirit, because the Spirit intercedes for the saints in accordance with God's will.
-Rom 8:27-

The Spirit himself testifies with our spirit that we are God's children. -Rom 8:16-

It doesn't matter who pray, we pray for the benefit of ourselves. But when we speak in tongues we pray for the benefit of God first.

"Please, do for me" can be compared to **"What can I do for you, the Lord."**

Matt 6:33-34, But seek first his kingdom and his righteousness, and all these things will be given to you as well.

As we see the scripture in 1 Cor. 14:14, **For if I pray in a tongue, my spirit prays,** the prayers of our spirit with the helps of Holy Spirit is very important, and "**my spirit** prays" is mentioned only in this place through the whole Bible!

d. We can pray for future events.

Here is an example of a true story in <u>Introduction of speaking in tongues</u> We can pray in tongues to prevent future accidents and dangers.

Also, I am going to quote a testimony mentioned by Rev. Kenneth E. Hagin in his book, "Tongues, Beyond the Upper Room."

One incident happened years ago when we had just started Prayer and Healing School on the RHEMA campus.

One day as I was ministering the Word, I had a sudden, urgent burden to pray, but I didn't know what to pray about. I asked "What is it, Lord? What is it?" Then I realized that someone's life was in danger. Someone was near death--not because of sickness or disease, but because of some kind of accident

So I got up and said to the crowd, "Folks, I have to pray, and I have to pray now. I am inviting you to help me pray. I don't know who it is, but someone's life is in danger." I knelt down and began to pray. I prayed hard and fast in other tongues and in groaning for about 45 minutes. Then I had a note of victory that let me know I'd prayed through. I sang and laughed in the Spirit, and that heavy burden to pray lifted. I said, "Well, I don't know who it is. Sometimes the Holy Spirit will show me the person or people I'm praying for. This time He didn't. But whoever it is, I got the answer, glory to God!"

That evening my wife and I invited our ministry singing group, Faith's Creation, over to our house so we could pray about certain matters. While we were praying, the telephone rang and my wife answered it. It was a young lady, a student at Oral Roberts University. She and her family were personal friends of ours.

The young woman said, "Momma just called from our home in Texas. She told me to call you and ask you to pray! There was an explosion this afternoon in the Texaco Refinery in Port Arthur, Texas!"

That was the division where the girl's stepfather worked. Due to the intensity of the fire, no one had been able to get into the refinery since the explosion, and quite a bit of time had passed,. (We figured out later that I got the burden to pray in the Spirit for someone in danger just about the time the explosion occurred that afternoon.) There were 17 men trapped in the refinery, and the rescue workers didn't know how many were injured or possibly dead.

When Oretha related to the rest of us what ;the young woman had said, I told my wife, "Tell her that we've already gotten the answer. Her stepfather is all right. The Spirit of God alerted us this afternoon to pray. Tell her we prayed through about it, and he is safe."

You may ask, "How did you know that this man and his coworkers were the people you were praying for in tongues?"

The Holy Spirit simply let me know through the inward witness as soon as I heard what had happened.

So my wife and I and the members of Faith's Creation went on with our business of praying about other matters. When Oretha and I finally got to bed, it was after midnight. About 1L30, the phone rang. It was the same young lady calling again. She told us, "Momma just called and said, "They finally got the fire put out--and when they went into the refinery, they discovered that not one person was hurt! They can't believe it! Every single person's life was spared! Daddy's fine!"

Thank God, the Holy Ghost knows what we are to pray for, and He helps us pray for the unknown!

e. Speaking in tongues gives a sign to un-believers.

1 Cor 14:22, Tongues, then, are a sign, not for believers but for unbelievers;

I read this story from a book long time ago, and cannot remember the name of the author.

It was a true story. An American G.I. stationed in Japan married a Japanese girl and came to his home town in Oregon. They went to his church on Sundays. While he prayed to God to convert his wife to Christianity, his wife also prayed silently in her mind,

"Blessed the name of Buddha."

She was a Buddhist. She was raised in a mountain village where a Buddhist temple was. From her early age she was Buddhist, and spent a lot of times in the temple.

One day, when her husband prayed fervently at his church, suddenly he started speaking in tongues.

Hearing the sound of his tongue speaking, his wife was surprised to death. He who didn't know Japanese, spoke a fluent Japanese language.

Furthermore, the language her husband spoke was not ordinary Japanese language, but special language used in Buddhist temple which only a few people understood. She was one of them who understood the language.

He prayed to God to show a sign for her, so she may believe in Jesus.

Of course, she believed in Jesus immediately.

f. The gift of speaking tongues draw other spiritual gifts.

Rev. C. S. Lee says that the gift of speaking tongue is as a magnet which can draws other gifts.

Generally when you speak in tongues, you could receive the gift of prophecy, and the gift of tongue-interpretation, and others.

Rev. Kenneth E. Hagin said, "To be filled with the Holy Ghost and to speak with other tongues is also the introduction to the gifts of the Spirit (1 Cor. 12-1-11).

I often say it this way,"

"Speaking with other tongues is the doorway into the supernatural realm of God. In other words, the infilling with the Holy Ghost and the practice of praying in other tongues on a regular basis is the doorway to all the other benefits and spiritual equipment that are ours."

Therefore, my brothers, be eager to prophesy, and do not forbid speaking in tongues.
-1 Cor 14:39-

People who speak in tongues prophesy easily.

The person who prophesy speaks in his own language (mother tongue). He represents for God, so some times, he uses "First singular" as pronoun.

The contents of the prophecy are advices, and reproaches to the church and church members.

When a person uses the gift of speaking in tongues continually, he can speak in different tongues.

Generally a person uses the gift fervently, God gives other kinds of gifts.

God does not give other gifts when one stop using the gift God had given him.

The Bible also encourage us to seek other gifts.

1 Cor. 14:1, Follow the way of love and eagerly desire spiritual gift...

g. We can have a proof of salvation.

One's spirit confesses his secret to God, and the Bible calls it, "speak in tongues."

When we speak in tongues, we certainly know that our spirits are **alive.** We have a definite proof that we were born again also. Some knows it by only faith. We know it by faith, but also by another proof, an audible prayer of our spirit.

> **The Spirit himself testifies with our spirit that we are God's children. -Rom. 8:16-**

Therefore the Christians who speak in tongues have their spiritual eyes open, and step into the spiritual world.

h. We can have very peaceful mind.

When we speak in tongues a lot, we can block the appearance of worldly spirits, man's bad images, and evil thoughts. After confessing sins searched by our spirit with the help of Holy Spirit, we can enjoy the heavenly peace our Lord promised.

We can keep only the image of Jesus, our Lord, the everlasting Peace.

> **Eph 4:2-3, Be completely humble and gentle; be patient, bearing with one another in love. Make every effort to keep the unity of the Spirit through the bond of peace.**

Also, the fruit of the Spirit is consists of "peace."

i. When we speak in tongues, we can pray for others who cannot pray.

People who have been in coma and "vegetative state" can understand 100% spiritually.

They cannot pray audibly.

Times to time God uses other people with the gift of speaking in tongues to pray for them.

At that time, the prayer is exactly the prayer they are supposed to pray.

God answers prayers and improves the conditions of the these people by giving them the conviction of salvation and faith. Then God takes them to heaven.

When we were doing missionary works in Puerto Rico, one day one Korean lady who married to a Puerto Rican man asked us to visit her father-in-law at a hospital for a prayer.

The problem was that he had been in coma for 3 years. When we arrived at the hospital, on the bed the man was shaking his head quickly side to side.

His son told us,

"it is useless to pray or to have a worship service, because he cannot understand at all, and he has only been shaking his head for 6 months."

We sang simple gospel songs anyway, and prayed aloud in tongues, and read Scriptures on salvation.

Then my wife whispered at one of his ears, "Jesus loves you, and do you believe Jesus as the Lord, don't you?"

To our surprise, he stop shaking his head side by side, and he nodded! Then less than one week, he passed away with the conviction of salvation.

God had waited for 3 years at the hospital in order to give him an eternal life!

Some people say that Speaking tongue is not important and they quote following scripture:

"But in the church I would rather speak five intelligible words (to instruct others) than ten thousand words in a tongue." -1 Cor.14:19-

People do not quote whole scripture. They omit the condition before speaking in tongues.

Condition is **"to instruct others."**

Suppose, there was a Sunday School teacher at the church of Corinth. He wanted to speak in tongues, and finally he got the gift of speaking in tongues. He was over excited, day and night he spoke in tongues. Finally he spoke in tongues when he taught Sunday School students.

Of course nobody understood.

So Paul wrote about the case.

Some ministers try to stop using tongues in their churches by quoting the scripture,

"If there is no interpreter, the speaker should keep quiet in the church and speak to himself and God."

If you read the contents of 1 Cor 14: 19, you know easily how the believers of the early churches had worship services. The contents of worship service are mentioned.

There were psalm, doctrine, a tongue, revelation, prophesy, and interpretation.

If there be nobody who can interpret the tongue, let keep silent during the worship service.

So, you may speak in tongues when you pray alone or together.

Therefore Bible says:

**Therefore, my brothers, be eager to prophesy, and do not forbid speaking in tongues.
-1 Cor 14:39-**

j. Speaking in tongues can give us spiritual refreshing

As long as we live in this world, some times we are spiritually down and easily contaminated. The best way to be refreshed is speaking in tongues until the peace and refreshing filled.

Therefore so many spiritual pillars have made themselves refreshed after mental, physical fatigue, turmoil, perplexity, anxiety, fear, and doubt.

Not only refreshing us, also speaking tongue in the Holy Spirit can build up ourselves.

Jude 20, But you, dear friends, build yourselves up in your most holy faith and pray in the Holy Spirit.

Rev. Stanley Howard Frodsham wrote in his biography: "The gift of tongues was a priceless treasure to him and many times every day his heart went out in love and adoration to God, not in the defiled languages of earth, but in the Holy-Spirit language of love that God had graciously given him."

He found that speaking in tongues was always a source of spiritual edification. He lived that verse in Jude 20.

CHAPTER 8

Reasons why people can not speak in tongues.

§

**1 Cor 12:30,
"...Do all speak in tongues?"**

Today, there are many Christians who do not speak in tongues.

You read the scripture above and try to understand the meaning clearly.

Why did Paul write this scripture? Because, only 10% of church members spoke in tongues at a church, or 80% of them spoke in tongues in another church. Either way, some church members did not speak in tongues.

The connotation of the contents tells me that most of the congregation in the church of Corinth spoke in tongues, but not all.

There are reasons why people can not speak in tongues today.

a. People who do not have the conviction of being born again, can not speak in tongues.

They are not genuine Christians.

In another words, people who do not have the Holy Spirit inside them can not speak in tongues.

The gift of speaking in tongue is the manifestation of the Holy Spirit.

First, we have to lead them to the Lord, and let them believe in Jesus, as their Lord and Savior by the help of Holy Spirit. Then they have the Holy Spirit inside.

Then they can be filled with the fullness of the Holy Spirit and can speak in tongues. The disciples who believed Jesus Christ as their Lord, and Savior by the Holy Spirit, received the fullness of the Holy Spirit at the Pentecost and finally they began to speak in tongues.

b. Christians who do not know anything about the gifts of the Holy Spirit, generally can not speak in tongues.

Giving the gift to the ignorant is as bad as giving a real machine gun to a small boy who does not know about the gun. We have to teach them about the gifts of the Holy Spirit, and let them understand clearly.

Therefore Paul recommended in 1 Cor 12:1.

Now about spiritual gifts, brothers, I do not want you to be ignorant.

c. Christians, especially leaders of the churches, who refuse and reject the gift of speaking in tongues can not speak in tongues.

Christians who like to receive better (?) gifts than the gift of speaking in tongues which they think the smallest, can not speak in tongues.

The gift of the Holy Spirit can not be compared with any gifts from the President of the nation.

Spiritual gifts are like flowers of a tree. Without flowers, there are no fruits. How can you get fruits without flowers?

Christians who do not have any spiritual gifts think they have the gift of love.

In the Bible there is no "gift of love". Love is the fruit of the Holy Spirit.

We have to teach them with the truth, and teach them humility. Then they can speak in tongues.

The Holy Spirit is gentle and respect the decision of Christians. When they refuse the gifts of the Holy Spirit, He respects their decisions.

If we are spiritually ignorant and do not know much about the gifts of the Holy Spirit, it is better to keep our mouth shut, because we can commit the unforgivable sin.

Matt 12:32, Anyone who speaks a word against the Son of Man will be forgiven, but anyone who speaks against the Holy Spirit will not be forgiven, either in this age or in the age to come.

Quite a Christian quote the following Scripture.

1 Cor 12:30-31, "Do all interpret? But eagerly desire the greater gifts. And now I will show you the most excellent way." -1 Cor. 12:31-

After this verse, Chapter 13 of Corinth starts.

This chapter is well known as **the chapter of love.**

The love is singular, and can not be plural such as **greater gifts** in 1 Cor. 12:31.

Paul mentioned a more excellent way how to use the gifts with "love" in Chapter 13.

Some Christians are afraid of receiving the tongues of Satan. If they had the Holy Spirit in them, they would speak in tongues given by same Holy Spirit.

d. Christians who believe that speaking in tongues ceased, can not speak in tongues.

They think the spiritual gifts ceased two thousand years ago, by quoting the scripture,

> **1 Cor. 13:8, "Love never fails. But where there are prophecies, they will cease; where there are tongues, they will be stilled; where there is knowledge, it will pass away."**

Paul stated that when Jesus (perfect one) would come, every thing would cease.

Did knowledge cease? No! Did hope cease? Of course not! Neither the tongues nor prophecies.

God is same yesterday, today, and forever.

e. Christians who try to receive the gift of speaking in tongues as a reward instead of a gift, can not speak in tongues.

Gift is free. Otherwise it is not gift. God can give his gifts to anybody, young or old, new believer or old one, illiterate or educated, holy or sinner according to human standard, and layman or leader.

His gifts are free. We cannot buy nor get the gift as the reward of our efforts or toils.

Normally, God gives His gifts to the humble.

Christians who acknowledge themselves as sinners, generally receive the gifts of the Holy Spirit easily than who think they are righteous.

The Grace of God flows downward, not upward.

We have to teach them to repent from their arrogance and to humble themselves.

Then they speak in tongues easily.

Peter and James both quoted same scripture,

"God opposes the proud but gives grace to the humble." -James 4:6, I Peter 5:5-

f. Christians who are full of evil ideas, worldly images, worries, sorrow, hatred, grudge, and egoism can not speak in tongues.

Normally these people can not pray in their mother tongues neither. Their prayers are completely blocked.

This is the worst case. They seldom speak in tongues.

At first, they have to sing hymns aloud a lot until they have peace in their hearts.

Secondly, raising hands in the air, clapping hands, or holding hands firm together with spirit filled Christians, can be recommended while they pray aloud for a long time. (30 minutes or more)

The prayer must be confessions of sins. It is good to write down the lists of sins committed from early ages remembered, then repent one by one.

When all sins are forgiven, they will feel the burden be removed.

Then they can ask the Holy Spirit fill them and give them the gift. They can speak in tongues easily.

The worst of the worst are who are addicted to sex, works, alcohol, gambling, and are involved in witchcraft, horoscopes, Roots, Tarot, psychics, hypnotism, and Ouija Boards, etc.

Some times the power (gift) of exorcism is required for the minister who can help people.

CHAPTER 9

Preparations for Speaking in tongues.

§

Then you will know the truth, and the truth will set you free." -John 8:32-

We feel uncomfortable and hostile against the truth because of our prejudice, barriers, bigotry, and lack of understanding.

a. I suggest you to read at least 5 times the following scriptures.

(1) Acts 2:1-12
(2) Acts 8:1-24

(3) Acts 10:1-48
(4) Acts 19:1-7
(5) 1 Cor. 12
(6) 1 Cor. 14

b. Think very simple.

God wishes us all speak in tongues.

Pray like this, "Heavenly Father, in 1 Cor. 14:5, you said that you wish, I would speak in tongues. So give me, Father, the gift of speak in tongues. In case I can not receive today, please give it to me tomorrow.

I don't deserve receiving the gift. But I know that it is free. If you give it to me today, I will appreciate it and will use it every day at least 30 minutes."

It is better to pray with loud audible voice.

c. Sing songs aloud.

Short songs are good, because you can sing them without looking at the hymnal, without reading musical notes and phrases, without distraction and have concentrated attention to God.

Repeat the song four or five times.

d. Before being laid on hands, repent all sins you remember now.

If you can not pray in your mother tongue, sing songs aloud until you feel peace in your heart.
 Then pray in your mother tongue with your hands lifted in air, or holding hands firm with a helper.

e. When a minister or a servant of God, lays hands on you, cry out aloud.

All of them were filled with the Holy Spirit and began to speak in other tongues as the Spirit enabled them. -Acts 2:4-

Who gave the utterance? The Holy Spirit did.
 Then who began to speak? People did.
 The Holy Spirit gives the utterance, but we should speak! I am pretty sure that the early Christians at the Pentecost were speaking in tongues aloud, because the people from different countries heard clearly and teased them as drunkards.

Let me give you an illustration of radio.

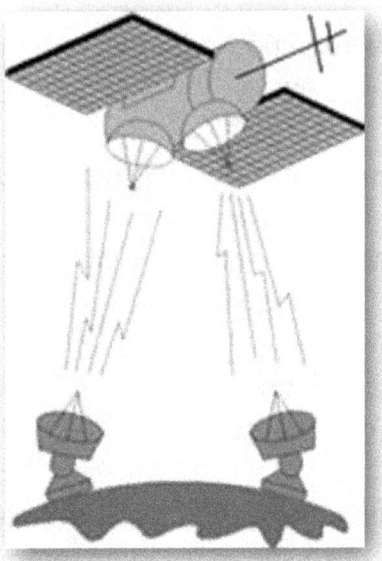

(a radio and broadcasting station)

If you like to hear a sound you have to turn on the switch. Likewise you have to open your mouth, using your tongue, and making a sound.

As long as you keep your mouth shut, you can not speak in tongues neither in your native tongue. Just like, you turn off the switch of the radio.

When the Holy Spirit (the broadcasting station) sends German language, the Christian (radio), sounds

German language. The sound of language is depending on the kind of language the Holy Spirit sends. The radio doesn't have any choice.

With one mouth you can not speak in two languages simultaneously.

In order to forget the native tongue, ministers suggest to shout "Hallelujah, Hallelujah, Hallelujah," or other words other than the native language.

It doesn't matter what you say, such as "Hallral", "Rolrol", "Coltal", "Pilal", "Tul", and "Cheel Ahahh", etc.

As long as they are not words of your native language, they will work. Forgetting your own language is the main point.

The leader of a coup d'état send soldiers immediately to three places almost without exception. He sends the soldiers to T.V. stations, radio stations, and newspaper companies.

Until he controls the tongues of the nation, the coup d'état can not be successful.

When children receive the gift of speaking in tongues, they don't need this kind of procedure.

After the delivery of the Gospel of salvation through Jesus Christ, and they sing songs together, and hold hands together, and with a loud shouting. With the prayer in tongues by the leading minister, normally 100% of all of children, begin to speaking in tongues. God is God of mercy, and love.

Children's faith is pure, and they believe what the Words of God promised about receiving the gifts of the Holy Spirit.

But no man can tame the tongue. It is a restless evil, full of deadly poison. -James 3:8-

The Holy Spirit likes to control 100% of the body, and uses His chosen language that is speaking in tongue. When He controls 100%, we call that state, "Full of the Holy Spirit, or the baptism of the Holy Spirit."

If the Christian shout in his native tongue, it is like playing cassette tape of his language at the same time trying to hear German language broad casting.

It is impossible to hear what cassette tape and of radio simultaneously. He must turn off the switch for the cassette tape in order to hear the radio broadcasting.

As long as he says in English, "Lord, I believe! Please, give me this today! Thank the Lord!" while expecting speaking in tongues, he cannot speak in tongues.

It is much better for him to shout and repeat "Halal, Halal, Halal,…….." the only half of the word, "Hallelujah." In Hebrew, which means "boast, or praise." So, it is quite OK to use the first part of

"Praise the Lord" in Hebrew. Say, "Halal, Halal, Halal, Halal,…………" aloud and repeat fast in order to forget your own language completely. When you say "Hallel, Hallel...", please don't make sound with some kind of intonation- pattern.

If you make some kind of intonation-pattern, your sound is controlled by your pre-determination. Your tongue still is controlled by your own thought of intonation-pattern, and not by the Holy Spirit.

When you sound "Halal, Halal, Halal……." aloud, as fast as you can, and repeat without intonation, suddenly your tongue would be twisted and strange sound come out of your mouth.

Then immediately stop saying "Halal, Halal...." and let your tongue say whatever it wants.

Now you may start to speak in tongues. Don't stop quickly. Speak aloud for at least 30 minutes or more.

If you like, you can pray for 2-3 hours. The longer is the better.

At the beginning of speaking in tongues, all start with confession of sins. That is why the most people cry with tears and runny noses.

Then they thank God for the gift, blessing, and His Grace. Then they thank God for their church and for the Kingdom of God, such as church revival, missions, and personal dedication.

I recommend Christians to speak in tongues for 30 minutes or more every day. They can speak in tongues when they drive, wash dishes, walk in a park, mow lawn, and do other things.

When they speak in tongues continually, God gives other tongues and other gifts.

If there is a minister with you who can interpret the tongue, his interpretation will encourage you and give you good assurance.

Some of you may think, "Why we have to prepare so many things?

Can the Almighty God do as He wants?" Uneducated people who do not have many theories, philosophies, worldly knowledge in their head, and have simple minds, can be filled easily with the Holy Spirit. But, well educated folks with complicated ways of thinking, and analytical minds, have a hard time believing in simple truth and they can not speak in tongues easily.

That is the reason why Jesus selected 12 simple fishermen as his disciples. People with simple faith, and pure hearts receive easily the gifts of the Holy Spirit.

Children with simple faith do not need these explanations and preparations. During worship with full of Holy Spirit, when a servant of God speaks in tongues out loud, all children can shout and pray together with the servant, then immediately they begin to speak in tongues.

Some folks are too complicate, and hardened to be filled with the Holy Spirit.

Therefore I mentioned in detail how to prepare for receiving the gift, step by step.

When they humbly follow the steps, God will let them speak in tongues. Praise the Lord!

CHAPTER 10

Deeper truths

a. Where do the gifts come from?

MANY CHRISTIANS THINK THE GIFTS come from the heaven.

In Acts 2, the Holy Spirit, came upon the people from the heaven as tongues of fire.

This was the first occurrence happened to the early Christians, so they believed that the gifts of the Holy Spirit come from heaven.

Today, many Christians think that way, and raise their hands in the air trying receive God's gifts from heaven. That is the expression of our desire, and readiness of receiving from God who is in heaven.

Some, including me, think the gifts come from the same Spirit who dwells inside us. The gifts are the manifestations of the Holy Spirit.

Christians full of the Holy Spirit will have the gifts of the Spirit.

When a Christian confess his sins, cleansing his mind and thoughts, dedicating himself 100% to the Holy Spirit, he will be filled with the Holy Spirit and will begin the language given by the same Spirit, which is the gift of speaking in tongues.

The Spirit himself testifies with our spirit that we are God's children. -Rom 8:16-

In Acts 2, as God promised the baptism of the Holy Spirit to the disciples first time in the history of mankind, God tried to show the event audio-video effects. They could hear the sound of a violent wind, see the tongues of fire.

God wanted them to remember clearly the historical event.

Acts 2 tells that the disciples of Jesus received the gift of speaking in tongues.

Acts 10 tells that unbelievers believed in Jesus and at the same time they spoke in tongues.

Acts 19 mentioned that 12 Christians in Ephesus believed in Jesus and were baptized in the name of Jesus.

Then they began to speak in tongues when Paul laid hands on them.

These are three different cases God wants to instruct us.

Old believers, brand new believers, and believers:
God is same, yesterday, today, and forever.
His principles didn't change either.
The Holy Spirit worked with old believers, brand new believers, and believers. He likes to give the gift of speaking in tongues to every Christian.
Our part is to confess our sins. When we confess our sins, God forgives. But, He can not do our part.
The first qualification for the servant of God is cleanness. If he keeps himself clean, God uses him regardless how big his faith is.

If a man cleanses himself from the latter, he will be an instrument for noble purposes, made holy, useful to the Master and prepared to do any good work. -Tim 2:21-

When we are clean by confessing sins, and dedicate ourselves 100% to the Lord, at that moment the Holy Spirit controls our tongues which are the most difficult part to be controlled, and lets us speak in tongues.

Then other gifts and fruits will appear naturally.

John 15 talks about a vine. Every branch that does bear fruit he prunes so that it will be even more fruitful.

Of course, true vine is Jesus, and branches are Christians.

Branches do not try hard to bear fruit. As long as they are connected to the vine, naturally they bring fruit.

To be connected to the vine, to be a part of the true vine, is very important.

The branches must have same quality, same purpose, and same life with the true vine.

If the branches have different quality, different purpose, and different life with the true vine, they will be cut off.

Today many Christians work hard, and try hard in order to bear the fruits of the Holy Spirit.

But they fail completely, or bear fake fruits. It doesn't work that way. We have to submit ourselves 100% to the Holy Spirit. We have to let Him manifest Himself through us and bear fruits.

b. Is there any direct relationship between salvation and speaking in tongue?

Some denominations that put too much emphasis on speaking in tongues say that without speaking in tongues there is no salvation. That is wrong. Their doctrine has caused a serious problems between denominations. Do they think that John the Baptist, the greatest among men born of women went to hell, because he didn't speak in tongues?

What a nonsense!

Bible clearly mentioned about this problem.

Therefore I tell you that no one who is speaking by the Spirit of God says, "Jesus be cursed," and no one can say, "Jesus is Lord," except by the Holy Spirit.
-1 Cor 12:3-

Only by the help of the Holy Spirit, we can believe in Jesus, as the Lord, and Savior.

By His help, we believe in Jesus, and are born again.

Let me give you an illustration. At our houses, we have air-heaters. During summer time, we do not turn on air-heaters. We do not say that the air-heater is dead as long as the pilot light is alive inside.

If the pilot light is out, we may say that the air-heater is dead.(or out)

All Christians have the Holy Spirit, as the pilot light, but do not set the thermostat high enough so that they are full of fire, the Holy Spirit.

As long as we have ashes, and debris of sins, world images, worries, and guilty consciousness inside the furnace, the fire can not work 100% effectively.

c. Interpretation of Speaking in tongues

For this reason anyone who speaks in a tongue should pray that he may interpret what he says.
-1 Cor 14;13-

Tongue interpretation is related with the secrets of the people, so God gives this gift to few people. Normally God gives it to the people who have the following merits.

(1) who speaking in tongues a lot
(2) who can keep secrets of others

(3) who is a leader of the church, who pray a lot for others, who can give good advices in order to benefit the church.

There are about 4 kinds of interpretations, I think.

(1) When some body speak in tongues, the interpreter hears in his native language.

   This kind of tongue interpretation gift doesn't last long. Sooner or later, he can not hear in his native language.
(2) The interpreters understand in his heart what the tongue speaker says. He can interpret a part or whole contents.

   Interpretation of tongues is different from the translation of languages.
(3) When the interpreter touches the head, back, or hand by his hand, he detect the feeling of the Holy Spirit through his own heart, and interpret the contents.
(4) When the tongue speaker pray, the interpreter prays simultaneously with the same tongue.

   That way the interpreter know the contents. This is the best way, and accurate way.

1 Cor 2:10-11;
But God has revealed it to us by his Spirit. The Spirit searches all things, even the deep things of God.

As I mentioned before, tongue interpretation is different from language translation.

In order to translate foreign language, you have to clearly hear the sounds and know the meaning of the words. Otherwise you cannot translate.

But tongue interpretation is completely different. When a Christian starts in speaking in tongues, in most cases, they speak in an inarticulate ways, repeat short sentences, or blurring sound.

But interpreter understand the feelings of the Holy Spirit, so he can interpret the prayer very clearly, beautifully, some times longer than the tongue speaker said.

Especially depending on the education, spiritual status, experience, and capability of verbal expression of the interpreter, the contents of the interpretations may vary.

d. Development of the gifts

Today, most churches in this world do not develop spiritual gifts given by the Holy Spirit.

Even though the Holy Spirit gives the gifts to the members of the body, the Church leaders do not encourage and help one another to make the whole body strong and healthy. Furthermore they are so ignorant that they despise, discourage, contempt, and are against any kind of spiritual gift..

They are supposed to encourage, develop, and use them wisely for the body of Jesus Christ.

Let me give you a good example.

An eye with a spiritual gift can see what normal people cannot see.

If the eye is being used in the place of hand, it is miserable moment for the eye and for the body as a whole.

Imagine, some one using his eyes in the place of hands. With eyes he pick up sour pickles. With eyes he washes clothes in the water with Clorox.

With same eyes he tries to install barbed wires on the fence.

Today, most of the churches do this way.

Church members are not satisfied. Rather they are agonized. The churches can not function properly as the body of Jesus.

Pastors of the churches should pray a lot for the members and find out their spiritual gifts by the help of the Holy Spirit. They must put the church members in right positions so they may develop their spiritual gifts, even some of them misuse the gifts of the Holy Spirit.

For this reason I remind you to fan into flame the gift of God, which is in you through the laying on of my hands. -2 Tim 1:6-

One day when I walked on the beach as usual, I was shocked by a revelation from the Lord, "Do you know what is the severe criminal act can be done by the pastor of a church? Wasting the spiritual gifts of church members for nothing! Use a member with the gift of prophecy as a parking guide, of healing or of miracles as church bus drivers!"

I don't say that the ministry of healing is greater than parking guide ministry.

If a father enforced his son work as busboy forever even he knew his son had a talent of violin and got a first prize at Tchaikovsky competition, what a cruel and bad father is for his son!

All the gifts of the Holy Spirit are more precious than any prize in this world, and using them in the proper place is very important and essential to the welfare, and growth of the body of Christ, the church.

e. Misunderstanding on prophecy

The gift of prophecy in 1 Cor. 12 is completely different from the prophecy made by prophets in the Old Testament.

Today some ministers try to stop the gift of prophecy by quoting the scripture.

> **If what a prophet proclaims in the name of the Lord does not take place or come true, that is a message the Lord has not spoken. That prophet has spoken presumptuously. Do not be afraid of him. -Deut 8:22-**

In the times of Old Testament, only prophets could prophesy. Their prophecies were about the warning to the country, and about the Messiah, Jesus Christ. Their prophecies were written in the Bible.

The prophecy in 1 Cor. 12 tells about a gift of the Holy Spirit, but we do not treat it as a part of the Bible. The purpose is completely different from the prophecy in the Old Testament.

> **But everyone who prophesies speaks to men for their strengthening, encouragement and comfort.**
> **-1 Cor. 14:3-**

The purposes of today's prophecy are for edification, exhortation, and comfort.

Mainly the prophecy is for the benefits of members or of a local church. The prophecy makes the arrogant humble, enhances the weak, and comforts those who are the down. The Bible encourages us to have the gift of prophecy.

> **Therefore, my brothers, be eager to prophesy, and do not forbid speaking in tongues.**
> **-1 Cor 14:39-**

> **Do not treat prophecies with contempt.**
> **-1 Thess 5:20-**

> **Do not neglect your gift, which was given you through a prophetic message when the body of elders laid their hands on you.**
> **-1 Tim 4:14-**

In the Old Testament, prophecies came from a few prophets chosen specifically for countries or people. The Words of God came to the prophet, and prophet's mouth was used as a tool.

They were chosen and used 100% by God's Will.

But, as you see in 1 Cor 14:39, "...be eager to prophesy", God encourages Christians to do so.

Furthermore, they can be numerous.

Why? In the Old Testament, the Holy Spirit came to certain people such as priests, prophets, and kings. But when they were contaminated with sins, the Holy Sprit left.

However, after the Pentecost, the Holy Spirit began to dwell in all Christians, and He doesn't leave us! He lives inside us, and will never leave us as long as we believe in Jesus Christ, as the Lord, and God.

Some times, the person who prophesies uses first person singular pronoun or quotes scriptures in the Bible. Some times, uses third person singular pronoun.

When he prophesies he use his own native tongue. Therefore his ideas, thoughts, and feelings can be added easily in his prophecy.

The contents are depend on his knowledge, faith, capability of expression, and purity of heart.

Therefore the Bible suggests to judge the contents. God knows his possible mistakes.

Also only in the proportion to his faith, he can prophesy. The pastor should judge the contents.

Two or three prophets should speak, and the others should weigh carefully what is said.
-1 Cor 14:29-

We have different gifts, according to the grace given us. If a man's gift is prophesying, let him use it in proportion to his faith. --Rom 12:6--

This prophesy is for a local church and church members who are in a particular situation.

Therefore it is different from the one in the Old Testament.

There are prophecies, they will cease:
-1 Cor. 13:8-

Then some may ask a question, "Then why do we need this kind of prophecies which can be wrong?"

Remember, the prophecies given by the Holy Spirit are always accurate.

Problem is that in the process of delivering the prophecies, prophets' thoughts and feelings are added accidentally.

Let me give you an illustration.

Near a river, there is a gold mine mountain, where many people try to collect small pieces of gold.

Some times they collect big pieces of pure gold.

It is a very good experience to find out the pure words of God in the prophecies by judging of sieving.

Even in the best diamond mine in the world, they have to collect diamonds from lots of dirt.

f. Misunderstanding on speaking in tongues

When we study the Bible carefully, we can find that there are two functions of speaking in tongues.

i) to edify himself
ii) to edify the church

Many of Christians use the gift of speaking in tongues to edify himself by praying and praising personally. But, tongue speaking has another function, edifying the church with tongue interpretation.

This case, this function is as good as prophecy and regarded as the words from the Lord for the particular church.

If you understand the two functions well, there will not be any dispute on the gift of speaking in tongues.

Today, the arrogance of tongue speaking Christians at church can cause all kinds of problems, especially misunderstanding of speaking in tongues also.

Can you figure out who hate the most and is against the gift of speaking in tongues?

It is Satan himself!

I am going to give you an illustration then you can easily understand the reason why.

There is a battle scene in Afghanistan.

One side, about one hundred of American soldiers are ready to fight against thousands of Taliban soldiers at the foot of the rocky mountains.

Their individual weapon and fighting power are the same.

Both sides have ammunition, grenades, etc.

But, among the hundred American soldiers there is a CIA man who has a special gadget, like an Apple I-phone.

He typed the exact location of enemy and requested helps from the headquarter.

Very soon, a few B-2 bombers came and poured thousand pounds bombs and killed almost all of enemy soldiers.

The person that Taliban soldiers hate the most is the CIA agent who has a secret weapon. The agent is able to make direct communication between him and the headquarter.

Speaking in tongue is a direct communication between a Christian, and almighty God.

Who hate speaking tongue the most? The enemy of God, Satan.

Satan tries hard to manipulate and agitate the minds of church members. That is Satan's tactic: to cause divisions and turmoil in the church.

g. Interpretation of 1 Cor. 14

Verse 1, "Follow the way of love and eagerly desire spiritual gifts, especially the gift of prophecy."

Paul suggests us to "follow after love." He means that love must be the motive, means, and purpose of the gifts.

The gifts without love are useless (1 Cor. 13).

In 1 Cor. 13, it is very meaningful to replace "love" with the word, "Jesus."

He commanded to desire spiritual gifts out of nine ones in chapter 12.

He especially recommended us to prophesy.

It seems like, Paul put this gift in first place among the spiritual gifts. Prophecy is very important for a church. It is God's special care for that particular church.

When a Christian speaks in tongues sincerely, some times he speak prophecy too.

Speaking in tongues and prophecy are like brother and sister.

Many people receive the gift of speaking in tongues and the gift of prophecy at the same time when they have the baptism of the Holy Spirit.

Verse 3, " But everyone who prophesies speaks to men for their strengthening, encouragement and comfort."

When church congregation hear the prophecy, they feel the presence of God immediately. They are comforted. They repent and rejoice in the Lord.

Verse 4, " He who speaks in a tongue edifies himself, but he who prophesies edifies the church."

Speaking in tongues edifies himself. Edification means to make better or to develop better. But prophecy benefits the church.

Think this way. Without speaking in tongues or prophecy, church members and the church can not be edified!

Verse 5, " I would like every one of you to speak in tongues, but I would rather have you prophesy. He who prophesies is

greater than one who speaks in tongues, unless he interprets, so that the church may be edified."

God likes to give the gift of speaking in tongues and also the gift of prophecy to every Christian.

If speaking in tongues is interpreted, it is as good as the prophecy or possibly better.

Verse 6-8, "Now, brothers, if I come to you and speak in tongues, what good will I be to you, unless I bring you some revelation or knowledge or prophecy or word of instruction? Even in the case of lifeless things that make sounds, such as the flute or harp, how will anyone know what tune is being played unless there is a distinction in the notes? Again, if the trumpet does not sound a clear call, who will get ready for battle?"

The above activities were the contents of worship service in the early churches including the church in Corinth. The orders and contents of worship service are different today.

Verse 9, " So it is with you. Unless you speak intelligible words with your tongue, how will anyone know what you are saying? You will just be speaking into the air."

Paul recommends the Corinthian church to speak in tongues with interpretation during worship service, and he prohibits the practice of the gift without interpretation.

Verse 10, "Undoubtedly there are all sorts of languages in the world, yet none of them is without meaning."

Paul emphasized that all sounds in the world have meanings. Furthermore, it is useless to say that (Unknown) tongues have meanings.

Verse 11, " If then I do not grasp the meaning of what someone is saying, I am a foreigner to the speaker, and he is a foreigner to me."

There must be a language that can communicate between two parties.

Verse 12, "So it is with you. Since you are eager to have spiritual gifts, try to excel in gifts that build up the church."

Today, how many Christians are zealous of spiritual gifts? Too many spiritual infants are at church only for baby-sitting.

They do not excel in gifts nor build up the church. Yesterday, and today, they are always babies.

Verses 13, " For this reason anyone who speaks in a tongue should pray that he may interpret what he says."

Today many Christians who received the gift of speaking in tongues give up using their gifts, because they do not understand the contents of the prayer between his spirit and God. They are 100% carnal Christians. They do not understand how important it is for their spirits pray to God. For this kind of carnal Christian, Paul raised a question and also answered that question.

Verse 15, " So what shall I do? I will pray with my spirit, but I will also pray with my mind; I will sing with my spirit, but I will also sing with my mind."

Paul suggested Christians to pray and sing with their native language and God-given tongues.

This way he can satisfy his soul and his spirit.

If the gift of speaking in tongues is ignored and not used, then why did God gives the gift?

A few years ago, a Chinese lady came to my wife's office. While she was sitting in a dental chair, testimonial conversation was going on between her and my wife. My wife asked a question, "have you ever spoke in tongues?"

She answered back. "Twenty six years ago, when I was young, I had an experience of speaking tongues at a revival meeting, but since that time I have never used. it"

My wife held her hands and prayed in tongues, and immediately the woman was filled with the Holy Spirit, and began to speak in tongues fluently and after dental treatment, she left the office with a renewed spiritual condition.

God doesn't take away the tongues he gave her.

Verses 16, 17, "If you are praising God with your spirit, how can one who finds himself among those who do not understand say "Amen" to your thanksgiving, since he does not know what you are saying? You may be

giving thanks well enough, but the other man is not edified."

When a minister tries to bless the congregation, suddenly a (unknown) tongue come out of his mouth, he should also bless with the language they understand.

Verse 18, " I thank God that I speak in tongues more than all of you."

Paul himself spoke in tongues a lot. He thanks God for it. Some times we hear ministers say, "I am not against speaking in tongues." You have to remember that they are neither or against it. Don't expect any encouragement from them. Actually, they are against the gift of speaking in tongues.

If they truly believe in the words of God, they do not have any choice except supporting and encouraging the gifts.

Lots of faithful Christians can speak in more than one tongue, and within a couple of months after they got the gift, they can speak more than one kind of tongue as long as they use the gift every day.

Quite a few times when one prayed for the gift of speaking in tongues, Christians began to speak in 3-4 different tongues during 10-20 minute periods.

Verse 19. " But in the church I would rather speak five intelligible words to instruct others than ten thousand words in a tongue."

Don't forget the words**, "to instruct (teach) others."** When you teach at Sunday School, do you need 5 words everybody understand, or 10,000 words of (unknown) tongue only your spirit and God understand?

Verse 20, " Brothers, stop thinking like children. In regard to evil be infants, but in your thinking be adults."

Today Christians in other ways, are men in malice and being children in understanding.
Without knowing the truth, they are easily against the spiritual gifts including speaking in tongues.

Verses, 21,22, " In the Law it is written:

Through men of strange tongues and through the lips of foreigners I will speak to this people, but even then they will not listen to me, says the Lord.

Tongues, then, are a sign, not for believers but for unbelievers; prophecy, however, is for believers, not for unbelievers."

In a service with many unbelievers God can use a Christian, and let him speak in tongues aloud.

They are surprised with the strange sounds from this man, and believe that God is working among them.

But when a person with the gift of prophecy stands up starts to say a prophecy, he cannot impress unbelievers. Because he uses the language they understand.

Unbelievers think he is talking from his thoughts.

The prophecy is for believers.

Speaking in tongues is a good sign for unbelievers.

Verse 23, " So if the whole church comes together and everyone speaks in tongues, and some who do not understand or some unbelievers come in, will they not say that you are out of your mind? "

Today in some small churches, all church members speak in tongues. In this scripture, we may see the possibility of speaking tongues by majority of the church members.

The first case happened, when the members of Jerusalem church spoke in tongues all together.

At that time people called them drunkards.

Today they call Christians mad.

Were they drunken? Are Christians mad?

No, not at all.

Then who call them mad?

The Bible says, the **unlearned** or **unbelievers** call tongue speakers mad!

Don't be afraid of the unlearned or unbelievers.

Don't pay too much attention to them.

If there is an interpreter, it is good for them.

Verses 24, 25, But if an unbeliever or someone who does not understand comes in while everybody is prophesying, he will be convinced by all that he is a sinner and will be judged by all, and the secrets of his heart will be laid bare. So he will fall down and worship God, exclaiming, "God is really among you."

Prophets prophesy in known language to an unbeliever, and about his secret revealed.

Then he will kneel down and will believe in God.

Prophecy can be used very wisely for evangelism.

Normally the gift of prophecy comes together with the gift of speaking in tongues or later.

Verse 26, "What then shall we say, brothers? When you come together, everyone has

a hymn, or a word of instruction, a revelation, a tongue or an interpretation. All of these must be done for the strengthening of the church."

Paul is talking about the order or contents of the worship service. In the program of worship service, there were a psalm, a doctrine, a tongue, a revelation, an interpretation, and prophecy.

Verse 27, "If anyone speaks in a tongue, two — or at the most three — should speak, one at a time, and someone must interpret."

Remember the maximum number allowed is three with interpreter during worship service.

Verse 28, " If there is no interpreter, the speaker should keep quiet in the church and speak to himself and God."

If there is no interpreter, speaking in tongue is not allowed during worship service. He can pray to God privately.

Verses 29, 30, "Two or three prophets should speak, and the others should weigh carefully what is said. And if a revelation comes to someone who is sitting down, the first speaker should stop."

Prophets should speak in order, only two or three during the worship service.

While a prophet speaks, the others listen and judge.

Suddenly a new prophecy comes through a person sitting, other prophets should give him priority. Because latest prophecy is most important one.

Verse 31, " For you can all prophesy in turn so that everyone may be instructed and encouraged."

In the early churches, there were many Christians who had the gift of prophecy.

Verses 32, 33, " The spirits of prophets are subject to the control of prophets. For God is not a God of disorder but of peace. As in all the congregations of the saints."

God is the author of peace. Therefore, the pastor or prophets can stop the prophecies in order to prevent confusion. Here is a difference between God's Spirit and Satan's spirit.

A demon possessed person can not control the works of evil spirit.

But God gave man free will. Man can control himself any time. Whenever he wants, he can speak in tongue and stop speaking in tongue.

The same principle is applied to prophecy.

Verses 37, 38, "If anybody thinks he is a prophet or spiritually gifted, let him acknowledge that what I am writing to you is the Lord's command. If he ignores this, he himself will be ignored."

What Paul wrote about spiritual gifts including speaking in tongues, is not his own, but the commandments of the Lord.

If some one doesn't understand and likes to stay ignorant, Paul suggested to leave him alone as ignorant.

The spiritual blind can not see!

Verse 39, "Therefore, my brothers, be eager to prophesy, and do not forbid speaking in tongues."

The words of God command us not to forbid speaking in tongues in the church, and to covet to prophesy. Today many church leaders stop speaking tongues in the church and reject prophecy.

What do you think about this according to the word of God? Do they work for God, or against God?

h. Author's own experience

From Korea the author came to Golden Gate Baptist Theological Seminary (one of six Southern Baptist seminaries) in order study theology for the Lord, about 47 years ago.

While I was studying at the seminary, I had a Korean friend, Mr. Buck who was many years younger than I was. His father founded a Korean Assembly of God church in San Francisco after his father became an ordained minister at the age of 60.

His father invited Dr. Paul (David) Cho who was pastor of the largest church in the world today, as the preacher for a revival meeting. Mr. Buck invited, me and Rev. Moon who is ministering in Tacoma, Washington and we went to the revival meeting at the week-end.

We were late and sit on the rear chairs. Dr. Cho preached a good sermon, and gave a special offer to the congregation at the end of the meeting.

He asked the people come out to front and kneel down along the isle and he promised he would pray for them.

Total participants were about 30-35. Most of them rushed to kneel in the front. I didn't have any experience of having laid hands on me. So I was sitting on a chair.

While every body received prayers, it was not appropriate to watch them. So I bow head down and prayed silently. A few minutes later I felt the hands of Dr. Cho on my head.

He prayed like this, "Heavenly Father, bless this young man. Use him wonderfully as your servant,…" I thought and said in my mind, "How can he know that I plan to be His servant? He has never met me. How on earth can he know about me?"

At that time I couldn't understand at all about his prayer and blessing. But now I know. The Holy Spirit let him know about me.

After the revival meeting the old pastor invited Dr. Cho and church members to the seminary apartment of Mr. Buck (his son). We were all in the seminary campus, so I participated in the cell-group meeting led by Dr. Cho. After the meeting Dr. Cho said, "Is there any question about being filled with the Holy Spirit or speaking in tongues?" I raised my hand, and asked a question.

It was about 10 months after I came to the Seminary as a foreign student. One night while I was sleeping, I heard a whirl winds coming into my ears and an unbearable fire and electricity filled my whole body, and my body became a fire ball. Few weeks later I had exactly same experience again. I didn't tell any body. So, I talked to Dr. Cho about this experience and asked him what the experience was. Immediately he told me that I was baptized by the Holy Spirit.

It was next Monday morning, after the early summer class, I was lying down on the couch in my apartment.

The morning sunshine was penetrating through the windows. It was one of the beautiful morning scenes in San Francisco bay area. In my logical thoughts, I said to myself, "if I was baptized with the Holy Spirit, I am supposed to speak in tongues.!"

Immediately my tongues was twisted and a strange sound came out from my mouth. I was surprised. I knew the Bible was truthful.

Not many friends around me spoke in tongues, and nobody encouraged me to develop the gift. So, I stopped speaking in tongues.

A few years later, while I was the pastor of a Korean church in San Jose, California, we had a revival meeting which was held without any previous schedule. God provided. It was 8 day revival meetings.

Every day we had two services, day break service and evening service. The speaker was Rev. Chun Suck Lee, one of the most powerful workers led by the Holy Spirit at that time. When he laid hands on church members, including the author, many spoke in tongues.

The author began to speak in tongues fluently.

While I drove my car in order to show Rev. Lee the sceneries of Bay Area, I continued speaking in tongues aloud with Rev. Lee at passenger's seat. On the way to the hill over Golden Gate Bridge, I was praying in tongues.

Suddenly Rev. Lee asked me a question,

"Pastor Seo, do you study at the doctorate program?"

I wondered how he could know that.

I said, "yes."

With a smile he said,

"Pastor Seo you have prayed in tongue like this, 'Heavenly Father, if you don't like me study for the doctorate program, I will quit the program immediately.' But it is good to finish the program. In this world you need the degree."

I was really surprised at his interpretation of tongues, and expressed my gratitude for his suggestion.

My wife and I have prayed in tongues aloud for decades. We spoke in many tongues.

When we pray together, many people received the gifts of tongues, and vision, including 5 year old kids.

From old men to young kids, all spoke in tongues when they wanted.

While we were working as self-supporting missionaries in Puerto Rico for one year, all people we prayed together received the gift of speaking in tongues.

Their lives were changed.

In South Korea where the largest churches of all denominations in the world are, there are many Christians who speak in tongues regardless denominations. The spiritual gifts of the people in Korea are the source of the power of the Christianity today.

We planned to go to Cuba as missionaries in June 1998, but the Cuban government didn't issue visa for us. So we stayed in Florida, waiting for the visa.

During this period, God sent Rev. Chun Soo Lee to lead a revival meeting at one of Korean churches in Miami area. We participated in the meeting. Rev. Lee is one of most spiritual persons in the world at that time.

He could find out the spiritual gifts of individual Christian immediately, and made a diagnosis of his spiritual status. He had interpreted thousand and thousand's tongues.

Through his revival meetings, I had been encouraged to write a book on speaking in tongues.

Because I fully understood the importance of speaking in tongues.

i. Other things in the Bible.

In the book of Job, we see the conversation between God and Satan.

What language did they use? Of course, heavenly language they used, because Satan was one of arch-angels in the heaven before he fell.

Satan and evil spirits have their own languages and communicate between evil spirits and their worshipers.

Their tongues have very strange sounds to spirit filled Christians, and make true Christians uneasy and uncomfortable, and some times fearful.

The language Paul heard on the way to Damascus could be Hebrew, Greek, Aramaic or Latin. The Hebrew people who accompanied with him couldn't hear the words from heaven.

One thing is very important. Paul heard the words clearly and understood.

The language Balaam heard from his donkey could be an animal language between donkeys, or Moab language. Which was it?

2 Peter 2:16 says, "But he was rebuked for his wrongdoing by a donkey--an animal without speech--who spoke with a human voice and restrained the prophet's madness."

One thing we should know that for God all things are possible.

Through many years spiritual life, my wife has had two unusual experiences.

My wife has a best friend, Dr. Choi who was a dental college classmate in Korea.

We heard her husband was hospitalized by a stroke and couldn't talk well and some times couldn't recognize people.

God allowed us to go to Seoul, Korea.

From the airport we went to the hospital directly.

We sang a short gospel song and read the Bible, and my wife prayed in tongue aloud for a while.

To my surprise, my wife asked Mr. Ko, her friend's husband if he could understand the contents of the tongue. I wondered, "Even he doesn't speak in tongues, how can he understand (interpret)?"

Because God asked my wife to let him answer.

I was surprised second time when he said, "yes!", and he told us the contents of the prayer in tongue.

God tried to show us that God can do all things, and try to boost our faith.

Similar story happened in Costa Rica while we did missionary work there.

In Costa Rica, there is a live volcano, and tourist are happy to go there. At night we can see red lava flowing down from the high mountain.

Some people go there by light-airplane tour.

One of Christians there asked us to visit a hospital, and pray for his brother.

This brother was a pilot of a tour airplane, and a few days before, his airplane collided on the mountain, and all the tourist were killed immediately except him. His major bones were all broken, and miraculously he was alive after long hours of surgery.

At the hospital, the pilot who didn't speak in tongues could interpret the contents of my wife's prayer in tongue. He became a good believer.

God can use a donkey to rebuke it's master Balaam.

Don't you think He cannot make you speak in tongues?

God loves you so much, he like to give you all gifts available to you.

James 1:17, Every good and perfect gift is from above, coming down from the Father of the heavenly lights, who does not change like shifting shadows.

Rom 8:32, He who did not spare his own Son, but gave him up for us all ?how will he not also, along with him, graciously give us all things?

God likes to give more spiritual gifts of the Holy Spirit when we pray in tongues diligently. The gift of speaking in tongues is lot better and important than the hot line between the president of USA and the president of Russia.

May God bless you richly, and I pray, and hope that you can grow spiritually a lot through the experience of speaking in many tongues and of other spiritual gifts.

Through this book, I hope many Christians can speak in tongues and live victorious lives in the Holy Spirit.

After reading this books, and experiencing the gift of speaking in tongues, as well as other gifts, please send me your personal testimonies to the following address.

Your testimonies will be used for the glorifying His name by sharing with other people.

Dr. John Seo, Ventura, California
E-mail: seofhibook@gmail.com
If your church needs help about this gift, please send me an e-mail.

About the Author

John (Fhi W.) Seo was born on Dec. 7, 1941 in South Korea.

After he had got B.E. (Chemical Engineering), he served his country as ROTC officer. Then he worked for Korea Oil Corp. as a chemical engineer for two years, then he got God's calling, and came to United States of America to study theology in 1968.

He got M. Div, M.R.E. and D.Min degrees from Golden Gate Baptist Theological Seminary, Mill Valley, California.

He had been ministering at Korean churches in California, including one Spanish Church. With his wife, a dentist they went to Puerto Rico as self supporting missionaries for one year, then for two years in & out, missionary works in Cuba and spent 3 years in Costa Rica. After returned to USA, they did Spanish missionary works in Santa Paula, Fillmore, and Piru, California for 4 years.

He has authored two books in Korean, and translated four books from English to Korean.

Reference Books

1. Speaking in Tongues by Jeffery Deaver
2. Speaking in Tongues: A Biblical perspective by Robert Lindfelt
3. Speaking in Tongues: Selected Poems by Charles Ghigna
4. Speaking in Tongues: Understanding the uses... by Harold McDonald
5. Speaking in Tongues by G. Hasel
6. Speaking in Tongues by Matthew Meyer
7. Speaking in Tongues by John R. Rice
8. Speaking in Tongues and Public Worship by Spiros Zodhiates
9. Speaking in Tongues by Napoli Rando
10. Receiving the Holy Spirit with the Evidence of Speaking in by Steve B. Walters

11. They Speak with Other Tongues by John Sherrill
12. The Speak in Tongues Controversy by Rick Walston
13. Speaking in Tongues: A Cross Cultural... by Felicitas D. Goodman
14. Speaking in Tongues by Joseph Dillow
15. Speaking in Tongues: Heaven's Language by Robert Engelhardt
16. Understanding Tongue speaking by C. W. Parnell
17. Speaking in Tongues by John McArthur
18. Speaking in Tongues: A guide to Research on Glossolalia by Watson E. Mills
19. So Your Wife came home speaking in tongues,.... by Robert Branch
20. Tongue Speaking: The History and meaning of Charismatic Exp.. by Marton T. Kelsey
21. Speaking in Tongues: Is that all there si by Bob Cook
22. The Spirit and his gifts; by George T.
23. Speaking in Tongues by Kurt E. Koch
24. Speaking in Tongues by Larry Christenson
25. The Hidden Power of Speaking in Tongues by Mahesh Chavda

26. Speaking in other tongues by Donald L. Barnett
27. Sounds of Wonder: Speaking in Tongues in the Catholic Tradition by Eddie Ensley
28. The Walk of The Spirit The Walk of Power by Dave Roberson
29. The Glory Within by Corey Russell
30. Life Lessons for a generation needs to hear by Wallace Hickey
31. The Gifts & Ministries of the Holy Spirit by Lester Sumrall
32. Filled with the Spirit by Joyce Meyer
33. The Power of Praying in Tongues by Glenn Arekion
34. The Baptism with the Holy Spirit by Oral Roberts
35. 70 Reasons for Speaking in Tongues by Bill Hamon
36. Tongues beyond the Upper Room by Kenneth E. Hagin

www.ingramcontent.com/pod-product-compliance
Lightning Source LLC
Chambersburg PA
CBHW071512040426
42444CB00008B/1606